T0062444

Cosmic

Warriors

—

PARTNERS

IN

The Ultimate Triumph of

God

By James Gibson

Order this book online at www.trafford.com
or email orders@trafford.com

Most Trafford titles are also available at major online book retailers.

Printed in Victoria, BC, Canada.

ISBN: 978-1-4269-2895-6

*Our mission is to efficiently provide the world's finest, most comprehensive
book publishing service, enabling every author to experience success.
To find out how to publish your book, your way, and have it available
worldwide, visit us online at www.trafford.com*

Trafford rev. 4/12/2010

 www.trafford.com

North America & international
toll-free: 1 888 232 4444 (USA & Canada)
phone: 250 383 6864 ♦ fax: 812 355 4082

Table of Contents

DEDICATION

To my wife, PAT,

<u>whose loving and faithful companionship</u>
throughout our personal and
spiritual journey together
has made this book
possible

and

To the memory of DR. NAT TRACY

friend and mentor of
the Faith

PREFACE

In January of 1965, I attended a mid-winter retreat, at the Howard Butt Family's Foundation ranch, near Leakey, Texas. I was a thirty-one-year-old minister participating with college students in four days of spiritual awakening. I was a pot full of proverbs, as described by Don Quixote when he interprets the mindset of his companion, Sancho, in the motion picture, "Man of La Mancha[1]." I was an assembly line seminary graduate wandering like a mouse in the maze of pastoral ministry. This was at the beginning of my career progressing toward becoming a mediocre Baptist minister.

Upon that retreat, I heard something that changed my life. I heard; "God knows that when life is given away, it returns in greater vigor than it was before. This kind of life is self-generating and self-sustaining. God's kind of life is the only life that is eternal by its nature, and God has invited humanity to participate in such life." When I first

---

1 *Man of La Mancha* tells the story of the "mad" knight, Don Quixote, as a play within a play, performed by Cervantes and his fellow prisoners as he awaits a hearing with the Spanish Inquisition.

heard this, something leaped within me and I said, "That is the most extraordinary thing I ever heard and I want to be part of it."

It was during this retreat that I felt the first urge to become a published writer. But, I did not want to write prematurely. It seemed appropriate to have something to say before writing. The first draft of *Cosmic Warriors—Partners in The Ultimate Triumph of God* was written in 1983 and 1984. Elton Trueblood, a prolific writer and president of Yokefellows International, critiqued the manuscript and said, "You have the making of an important book, but it must be recast entirely if it is to be a successful publication."[2] It has been recast entirely, but unfortunately the late Elton Trueblood is no longer available to confirm whether I have adequately completed the "arduous task of recasting." Others, like your selves will need to make that evaluation, but now I feel confident that I write with something to say.

In the final scene from the motion picture, "Man of La Mancha", when Cervantes is summoned to appear before the Spanish Inquisition, the Governor, a big, burly, but good-humored criminal who presided over the prisoners' mock trial of Miguel de Cervantes, returns to Cervantes his manuscript and says, "Read as well there as you did here and you may not burn." Cervantes replies, "I have no intention of burning." Transposed, the Governor's message to Cervantes says to me, "James, write well and you may not burn." A voice within whispers, "I have no intention of burning."

Cosmic Warriors—The Ultimate Triumph of God is my story. It is not memoirs, but a tale that must be told.

James Gibson
Bangs, Texas
Wednesday, 01-27-10

---

2   Elton Trueblood: From his critique letter dated March 29, 1985.

INTRODUCTION

Astronauts selected the top ten photographs taken by the Hubble telescope during its journey. The Sombrero Galaxy, pictured upon the front cover of the book and officially called M104, was voted the best picture. The Sombrero Galaxy is 28 million light years from Earth. It has 800 billion suns and is 50,000 light years from one side to the other. In comparison to the Universe, our planet, Earth, is an insignificant speck of dust. Yet, our planet has been selected as the arena for the resolution of the greatest issue in the Cosmos; "Whose kind of life deserves to be supreme?" This question will not only be resolved upon planet earth, but the family of God has been selected to become partners with God in bringing this question to its resolution. We marvel at the grandeur of our universe, but even more marvelous is the proposition that humanity has been invited into the family of God to partner with Him in ordering and bringing the cosmos to its fulfillment. Wouldn't it be foolish for people to make worldly enterprises the focus of their lives, when such magnitude invites us? Wouldn't one's indifference or rejection of this purpose for their life constitute their greatest sin?

This book is being written for those adrift in a sea of spiritual and institutional deadness. Some are drifting aimlessly, treading water in a life vest, and waiting for death to release them to live another kind of life. Others are fruitlessly flailing the deadness, but getting nowhere. I hope this book will become a life raft for all to clamber into and be carried to real life. Also, I am writing for all those who feel there must be more to God's enterprise than living forever, floating upon clouds, and lounging around heaven with nothing to do. If you are one of those who sense a need for additional spiritual growth and development, this book could be for you.

In this book we will be seeking to comprehend the character of God. Why does God's character seem to be just beyond our grasp? Could it be that it is because God is an ever-expanding being? Those scriptures, which imply that God never changes, may be saying that God is not a static being, but a God who will never cease to increase.

Another purpose of this book is to define a way leading from unawareness, or indifference, toward participation in God's quality of life. Adventurers upon this pilgrimage will journey toward becoming Cosmic Warriors who fight battles and win wars in this world and eventually in eternal enterprises, which eyes have not yet seen or ears heard. Jesus is our physical demonstration of God and He is the first among many of His same kind. Shouldn't those who follow Him recognize their need to embody the same kind of life He demonstrates, if not in total, then at least in kind.

The thread that runs throughout this book is that God has bound His ultimate triumph to the ultimate triumph of His family, for this is the kind of servant life that God has chosen for Himself. This means that the ultimate triumph of God waits upon the development of Cosmic Warriors who have the quality of life to overcome in the world and worlds beyond. But first, we must find the way to such life and travel upon it.

Would you like to see beforehand where the writer is going? Chapter one highlights the weakness of contemporary Christianity in its failure to call Christians to their destiny, which is to become God's people who can participate in God's kind of life. We shall never be equal to God, but we can be like Him in kind. Chapter two highlights the need to go on a voyage (pilgrimage) if we are to reach such a destiny. Also, in chapter two, readers are introduced to the nature of the journey, which is like getting into a boat and carried along by a stream to our destination. The next five chapters deal with elements of the stream that carry us on this voyage. The elements of that stream are: Captivation by the character of God, spiritual bankruptcy, commitment to Godlikeness, learning how grace operates to put away our Sin, and submission to the authority of God. Readers should note that when Sin is capitalized, it denotes the broken nature within us that causes us to commit sins.

The eighth chapter describes arenas of life in this world for Cosmic Warriors to venture into and conquer. Some of these arenas are: marriage, business and vocation, labor-management relationships, and the church. These are practical and natural arenas for the expression of the new life that our voyage carries us into.

The final chapter declares that voyagers, who take this journey, will find themselves endorsing a body of truth upon which their lives will be built. Listed within this chapter are suggested individual truths, which will sustain those in the journey and propel them to believe in the ultimate triumph of God.

The impact of authentic Christians, living servant lives, will do more to establish a true understanding of authentic Christianity than all the words in this book. Yet, I feel compelled to write them down.

CHAPTER 1

ABUSIVE RELIGION

"Make not my Father's house an house
of merchandise"
(John 2:16 c, KJV).

Judaism was abusing people when Jesus arrived in the world, but they were not aware of their apostasy. Could contemporary Christianity be doing the same thing without being aware of it? As volatile as the prospect seems, contemporary Christianity needs to evaluate itself with an open mind. There were good and bad priests and religious people during Jesus time on earth. There are good and bad Christian ministers and churchmen during our time. However, there could be as much need for an honest self-evaluation now as there was then.

The following story illustrates abusive religion in Jesus' time.

* * * * *

"I'm glad Feisty was turned down. We didn't know he had that wart behind his ear. He couldn't help it. But, I'm glad anyway."

These were the musings of Mark, a nine-year-old Jewish boy, as he sat in the outer court with his mother, younger sister, and baby brother. His father and a priest were sacrificing their lamb. Mark had gone with his father to the temple earlier. They carried Feisty in their arms. Feisty was special. They had selected him from their flock weeks ago. He didn't have a name then. Feisty was the name which best suited itself to his nature. He was a pest who stuck his head into everything! He worried and tickled the baby, trying to make nipples out of fingers and toes.

"Father says," mused Mark, "Feisty is our best lamb. He is, too! I don't care what that old priest said! He's just as good as that kosher lamb we bought!"

Mark's father was a hard-working homebuilder who did not have much money. It took careful management to meet his family's needs. He was concerned not only about their physical needs but about his family's spiritual needs as well. He was glad they could go to the temple and offer their sacrifice. Mark's father understood how it would affect Mark to sit in the outer court while he and the priest killed and sacrificed their lamb. He remembered how the sacrifice had first affected him as a boy. He knew that Mark would try to be a better boy just as he had tried to be better when he was growing up.

Mark's family returned from the temple where their sacrificial lamb had been offered. As was the custom, they began to prepare the meat of the lamb for their family meal. Their emotional soil had been plowed deeply.

That evening, as the family gathered around to eat their meal, they began to talk about matters that were important to them. Mark's father said, "We must try to care for each other. Let's try not to hurt each other." His eyes moved toward his wife, and she returned a look of understanding and complete agreement.

Mark asked, "What is God like?" Mark had been wondering why innocent lambs must suffer for people's sins. His father's answer did not satisfy Mark. Mark coaxed further, "Why did they reject Feisty?"

"He had a wart behind his left ear," replied his father.

"But the kosher lamb had a mole on his stomach. How much did the kosher lamb cost?" asked Mark.

"Fifty dollars," replied his father.

"Why do they cost so much?" continued Mark.

"Because they are kosher!" exclaimed his father.

Mark's father was uneasy with Mark's juvenile inquisition. Like many other fathers, he thought Mark was too young to understand why religious people often behave in an uncomplimentary way. Mark's father wished that religious life was different, too, but what could he do? Like so many other people, he reasoned that some things must be accepted even if you do not prefer, understand, or accept them.

Mark's father was certainly more disturbed than he dared show. When he had gone to buy the kosher lamb, he had been required to make his purchase with temple money—the currency of exchange within the temple. The exchange rate was two Roman dollars for each temple dollar. He had given the moneychanger one hundred Roman dollars in order to get the required fifty temple dollars. Then he sold Feisty to the cull buyer outside the temple and was paid market price, which was twenty-five Roman dollars. This year's sacrifice had cost him seventy-five Roman dollars and a prime lamb. Each year it was getting more expensive to be religious.

Later, Mark came running and shouting, "Daddy, I saw Feisty; he's in the kosher pen!"

* * * *

We have little difficulty recognizing the weakness of New Testament Judaism. Jesus made the anemia of their religion painfully obvious, which became a primary reason for their determination to eliminate Him. Do we see clearly the weaknesses of our own Christian religion? Dr. Nat Tracy, in his recently published manuscript, "A Search for Authentic Christianity," poses this question: "Have we come dangerously near to missing authentic Christianity?"[3] Just as Judaism became gradually sedated to horrible religious offenses committed against people, we may have become sedated to abusive religion that is less than authentic Christianity.

Perhaps Mark was there when Jesus made a whip and drove these abusive religious people out of the temple. Mark would have smiled, perhaps even laughed, when Jesus did this. Jesus could not accept or ignore the abuses of anemic religion. He was angry, as He should have been. Do you cringe when you hear Mark's story? Do you become angry when abusive religion depersonalizes people making them to be objects for others' purposes? Isn't this denying people's individual worth and rendering them to be pawns upon another's playing table? Isn't it a terrible thing to distort the image of God, which people hold, for consciousness of God is the fabric from which a culture derives its moral fiber?

Religious abuse rips off people and prejudices the minds of children against God. The inevitable result of anemic religion is the moral decay of a culture. If this is true, then we have a dependable thermometer to measure the quality of our nation's religious life.

Let's look at what has transpired in Christian history.

---

3   Nat Tracy, *A Search For Authentic Christianity.* Revised, Rearranged, Updated, Edited by Dr. Gary Manning p1. (Trafford Publishing 2009.)

EARLY CHRISTIANITY

In 125 A.D., Hadrianus, the emperor of Rome, asked Aristides, a renowned philosopher, to critique the world's religions. Perhaps Hadrianus wished to endorse a religion that could enhance his reign. After describing various world religions, Aristides responded to Hadrianus with these words, "But the Christians, O King, while they went about and made search, have found the truth; and as we learned from their writings, they have come nearer to truth and genuine knowledge than the rest of the nations."[4] After a long description of their manner of life, Aristides concluded with the summary: They love one another. They never fail to help widows; they save orphans from those who would hurt them. If they have something they give freely to the man who has nothing, if they see a stranger, they take him home, and are happy, as though he were a real brother.

Does Aristides description of early Christianity still fit modern Christianity? Or, has something transpired in the past centuries, that has changed contemporary Christianity? If it has changed, then what could have made the difference? Lets look at some possible occurrences that could have made a difference.

GROWTH PAINS

Early Christians, captivated by the character they saw and touched in Jesus, with excitement and enthusiasm, set forth to propagate His good news. Yet, their own spiritual growth and development was not complete and they made early mistakes. Judas' betrayal, Peter's denial, James and John trying to use Jesus for promotion of their agendas

---

4   The Apology of Aristides the Philosopher (around the year 125), from section XV.

and Thomas' doubt were just visible tips of the iceberg and the first signs of difficulty in this budding bungling movement.

After Pentecost they became enamored with growth, which gradually displaced their assignment of discipleship. Paul and Peter both baptized entire households when the head of a household embraced Christ. Early Christians emanated vibrant life, which attracted the spiritually hungry, the curious, and status seekers, who were added without caution to their numbers. It was inevitable that early churches would become boiling pots of conflict and dissent. Paul wrote much of the New Testament trying to quell these outbreaks of departure from authentic Christianity and frequently warned in his letters about clever, lying teachers infiltrating the Christian community. Peter, James, John, and the writer of the book of Hebrews joined Paul in writing books, now comprising much of our New Testament, which were primarily designed to correct, encourage, and guide early Christians toward a better demonstration of Christianity.

During the first two centuries, the early church experienced such phenomenal growth that in 325 A.D. Constantine established Christianity as the Roman Empire's State religion. Christian leaders rejoiced and raised little if any objection to soldiers and bureaucrats being declared members of the Christian church. There was little commitment to the life of Christ and allegiance to Him within this added numerical growth. Christianity was viewed as the wave of the future, and wave riders jumped upon the best wave of the millennium. Such explosion of growth is frequently viewed with awe. However, this unbridled growth may have crippled Christ's church and triggered departures that continue even to the present.

While this exploding growth was occurring something else was happening—Christian ideology was being compromised.

COMPROMISED IDEOLOGY

As Christianity moved from its Eastern roots toward Western cultures, it began to incorporate Greco Roman philosophies with its Christian theology. For instance: the concept of man held by Plato and other Western philosophers, called Platonist, replaced the Eastern thought of man as a unity of body, mind, and spirit, (Judaism and Christianity both had their origins in cultures with Eastern mind sets). Platonism defines man as a being having a body, mind and spirit. As similar as this may sound, it is contrary to the Eastern concept of man. There is a difference between thinking we **are** a unity—body, mind, and spirit and thinking we **have** a body, mind, and spirit. Under Platonist thinking, man is not a unity, but man becomes a trichotomy. As a trichotomy, people can give their spirit to God while retaining the rest of themselves for their own purposes. So, Christianity evolved into a religion composed of many people who give their souls to God for safekeeping and then live otherwise as they please. This opened the door for partial commitments and this basic flaw has been a crippler of Christianity in Western cultures.

In contrast, Eastern religions solicit a deeper commitment from their followers. This is why Islamic people—sacrificing their lives in terrorist actions—frighten, surprise, and puzzle those in the West.

Because of this mingling of philosophies, original Christian ideology became contaminated, and the door to partial commitment was opened. Could this be the reason that Great Britton and now America are fast disqualifying themselves as the banner bearers for authentic Christianity? Those who watch world Christianity, anticipate a new banner bearer. Who will be the new Christian leader? I saw impressive Christian commitment in Africa, where Eastern thought and Western thought coexist. Africa could be the continent out of which God will enlighten His world. Wouldn't it be just like God to enlighten and accomplish His purpose for the world through what some call the Dark Continent? Others see China as the possible new banner bearer. The Chinese still hold to the Eastern concept of man as a unity—body, mind and spirit. Does it grieve you to think that Christianity in Western cultures is losing its opportunity to enrich our own people and the rest of the world by our inability to establish and demonstrate authentic Christianity?

Growth issues and compromised ideology are not the only reasons why our Christian religion is having difficulty; there is the additional challenge of institutionalization.

INSTITUTIONALIZATION

Add to the above scenario the influx of institutionalization and you have a formula for disaster. Jesus once said to His disciples, "Take heed and beware of the leaven of the Pharisees and of the Sadducees" (Matt. 16:6 b, KJV). Apparently, Jesus feared that institutionalization, which had robbed Judaism of its vitality, would become a threat to His followers. Otherwise, He would not have warned them against it.

Leaven in dough works very slowly and silently so one is hardly aware of its presence. But, eventually its effect can be seen. Could it be that without knowing it, we have traveled the road of institutionalization?

When churches become institutionalized, the life of the institution becomes more important than the lives of people. When an institution becomes primary, people are overlooked, overrun, and a 'gospel' evolves that fits this point of view.

There was a woman whose experience well illustrates this truth. She gave herself faithfully to the church for more than sixty years. She had a thirst for God and longed to be nearer to Him. She made rededications of her life in efforts to satisfy her inner restlessness. Her church gave her positions of leadership, but this did not satisfy her deeper needs—it only satisfied the church's need for organizational strength.

She was in turmoil within. Her father had been a strong disciplinarian who ruled his household by the volume of his voice. She had grown up in his house gritting her teeth and swearing that when she married there would not be a man ruling over her. She tried to usurp the masculine role in her marriage and became manipulative and domineering. It became an infection to her marriage and a wedge of separation between herself and her son.

The churches to which she gave herself were not geared to lead their people to journey within, discover themselves, and present their broken beings to God for healing. She died in her eighties without ever receiving help. She became the victim of religion, which is most concerned with its own life instead of being concerned about the lives of its people.

Churches, enamored by numerical growth alone, with compromised ideology, and driven by the need to satisfy the purposes and needs of their own organization, will reduce human personality to the sum of one to be added to and counted as grist for the institution's mill. Such behavior is personality murder that will do great harm to humanity.

A young woman in a retreat lamented: "I felt a need for relationships. I was lonely and felt rejected and isolated. I sought for a church to meet the longings of my wounded spirit. I visited several churches hoping to find the one that was right. One of those churches responded enthusiastically to me. They visited me and reached out to me. After I joined that church, no one seemed to care about me any more." Then, with tears in her eyes she asked, "Doesn't anyone love and care about me?"

Growth pains, compromised ideology and institutionalization are not all that is plaguing contemporary Christianity for there is the added dilemma of incomplete reformation.

INCOMPLETE REFORMATION

There is a prevailing belief among many Christians that the Reformation took care of all the inadequacies of the church. The Reformation just scratched the surface of needed renewal. The Reformation is not a completed event, but it is an ongoing event that continues until the present.

In recent years we have seen the emerging role of the laity in Christian ministry. These awakened laymen and laywomen have discovered the priesthood of all believers and are exercising their roll and calling as ministers. This is evidence of the continuing growth and development of the reformation.

The continuing Reformation proves that the church is really a living organism like our human bodies, not just an organization—even though the church does have and requires organization. Yet, this living organism has the kind of life within it, which has the capability of healing its self. The renewal that is needed is not a new movement; it is the jump-start of the Reformation that has already begun. The church, as a living organism, is going to eventually find the resources within to heal its self. Like our human bodies, which will not tolerate invasive foreign bodies—the church will eventually automatically reject intolerable invasive departures. Resistance to renewal is going to eventually lose in the struggle. Revitalization in the church is going to happen. The only issue is—when will it happen?

If Christians could honestly see our apostasy as clearly as we see Judaism's apostasy, there should be a repentance deep enough to produce willingness to embark upon a journey that leads to renewal. But, will Christians ever see themselves honestly? Jesus exposed Judaism's anemia by being the Truth laid down beside their lie. True, it ended in His crucifixion. Then, following the resurrection, Jesus left His work in the hands of His followers. Can it be possible that out of anemic Christianity, vital Christians can rise to become the Cosmic Warriors who do for our religion what must be done? Upon a first look, it appears hopeless. Yet, it isn't. God has initiated the seemingly impossible assignment of taking broken twisted people and making them to be His sons and daughters. It is possible that when God looks upon humanity, He sees Messiah like material.

The sixteenth chapter of Matthew says, "One day the Pharisees and Sadducees came to test Jesus' claim of being the Messiah by asking Him to show them some great demonstrations in the skies." Jesus tells these religious questioners that they want a sign, but no sign would be given to them except a miracle like the miracle that happened to Jonah.

What was that miracle? We see the miracle as a runaway prophet being thrown overboard, swallowed by a big fish, and then vomited upon shore. It is commonly interpreted that the miracle of Jonah was surviving in the belly of the whale—ordinarily expected to become a dead man—then being miraculously cast alive upon the shore. Was that the primary miracle? It certainly pictures the death, burial and resurrection of Jesus, which is proof that He is the Messiah. But there is the possibility of another miracle proving that Jesus is the Messiah.

The other miracle was an undeserving, unwilling, and rebellious prophet, bringing God's message to unruly people and having a good response. The church will recover its vitality when there is a miracle like that. For when broken and undeserving followers of Jesus find a way to do for our church and world what Jesus started, this will also be proof that Jesus is the Messiah.

Jesus tells the disciples that he will take stones like Peter and fashion a body, which will be indestructible, a body that will pattern the world after heaven and blow the gates off of hell. In view of the above, my hope is revived that there is still the possibility for Western Christianity to arise to the challenge and become God's people mirroring His likeness to the world. These vital Christians will become the Cosmic Warriors accomplishing God's purposes in this world and in the worlds to come.

But, what will happen if Christians continue their apostasy?

IF CHRISTIANS CONTINUE THEIR APOSTASY

Hemmingway in his book, *The Old Man and the Sea*, writes the story of an old man who makes his livelihood as a hardworking fisherman. He is a good man who uses his resources to help others, like a boy who needs encouragement and assistance. He pays the boy to help him pull his boat ashore even though such assistance is not necessary. He will on occasion take the boy out to sea with him and pay him for unnecessary help, but the old man enjoys the boy's companionship.

The old man dreams of someday catching a big fish which will enhance his reputation and boost his economic condition. The day finally arrives when he has such a fish on his line. The fish fight lasts for parts of three days and all of two nights. He is carried far out into the sea by the fish. When the fish is subdued and secured alongside his boat, the old man begins the long trip back to shore. He worries that sharks will attack his catch. A shark strikes the fish and wounds it deeply, but the old man valiantly fights the shark and wins his right to keep his catch. But the wounded fish begins to leak a blood trail for predator sharks to find and follow. The sharks arrive in numbers and strip his catch of all but the skeleton.

In the economic sea, there are predators who live off the productivity of others. That scenario is the underlying theme in the movie, "Pretty Woman," with Richard Gere and Julia Roberts. Viewers of this motion picture may first conclude that Vivian, portrayed by Julia Roberts, who is a Hollywood Boulevard prostitute, is the one having a lifestyle problem. However, as the story progresses, it is revealed that Edward, portrayed by Richard Gere, who is a wealthy and powerful entrepreneur, uses his power to bankrupt individually owned mega businesses, buy those businesses at reduced prices, and parcel them to others for profit. This produces nothing and contributes nothing to the well being of the world. It only takes advantage of the opportunity to make money. Such entrepreneurs take but do not give. They pride themselves in their ingenuity and affluence, but they are bloodsuckers and parasites, living from the productivity of others. Viewers of the movie can easily see that economic predators like Edward have a much worse lifestyle problem than prostitutes, like Vivian.

If Christians continue to falter, economic parasites will continue to prosper and increase. Eventually, this kind of people will destroy economic affluence. They will consume and waste the resources of a nation and the world. This has been noticeably demonstrated in more recent factors in our present economy—governing bodies, banking, residential construction, the petroleum industry, and automobile industries.

Is this the kind of world in which you would choose to live? Is this the kind of life that is going to prove itself supreme? Can renewed Christians forming a vital church, with spiritually mature members, prevent the disaster described above? Already, tremendous good comes from seemingly inadequate Christianity—Education, health care, evangelism, childcare, family care, missions, and ministries to the poor and dysfunctional flow out of the Christian religion. If all this good can flow from seemingly inadequate churches, what might happen if there were vital life-pulsating churches? Christ's church, with many of its people revitalized, could march shoulder-to-shoulder against humanity's adversaries and become the Cosmic Warriors ordering this world and eternal regions beyond. In the pages that follow, let us see if we can find a way leading to such ultimate triumph of God.

CHAPTER 2

A VOYAGE

"Must I forever see this sin and sadness
all around me?"
-- Habakkuk 1:3a

I grew up on a farm in rural Texas, the youngest child in my family and the only boy. My sisters were 10 and 8 years old when I was born. There were no children in the area with whom I could play, so I was lonely and wishful for a little brother to be my companion. The wished-for-brother never arrived, but when I was nine years old, my oldest sister came home to give birth to her first child, a baby boy. This was an answer to the longings of my heart, and I bonded with this baby. I was unaware of a health condition that would not allow Ronnie to live. He lived for a month, and when I came home from school one afternoon, I was told, "The baby is dead." This was a devastating event in my life. The pain of losing someone that I loved created havoc in my young life. I unconsciously resolved to never love anyone this deeply again and began to build a wall of separation to protect myself from such trauma. I became reserved, reclusive, and, like a rock skipping across a pond, I could only touch people on the surface, never settling down to sink deeply into relationships.

In combination with this experience, there were other unsettling events, which resulted in fearful feelings and sleep disturbances. I experienced nightmares, sleepwalking, and crying out in my sleep. My youngest sister, who was seventeen years old, came to my bedside one night to ask, "James Carl, what is troubling you?" I replied, "I don't know." She continued, "Is there anything that I can do?"— To which I replied again, "I don't know what can be done." She asked, "Do you ever pray to God?" I answered, "I don't know how to pray." She responded, "You talk to God just as you talk to any person." So, I began a dialogue with God when I was nine that has continued for 66 years. This was the beginning of my voyage.

Those early cries to God were mostly cries for help. Having a sister who loved me in my home, and having God to talk with brought some relief; however, asking for the ability to really love again would come years later and it would not come quickly or easily. But, when I was thirty-four years old, I found myself loving a little girl who was dying with leukemia. It was a love that arose from deeply inside me that I could not have summoned at will. I could not allow her to die without loving her, and I realized that I was glad that I had loved Ronnie, even though loving him had caused great pain.

In the years that have followed I found myself loving again and again with a love that spirals higher and higher. Something has been taking place within me that was beyond my human capabilities. It was something that only God could accomplish. Yet, in my continuing dialogue with God I hear Him whispering, "This is just the beginning."

Who am I? What is my destiny? What is God like? These are questions that many people ask. When we ask such questions, we become thinkers, and when we think, we become philosophers, for to stop thinking is the only way to avoid philosophy. The real issue is—how good is our philosophy? So, would you think with me for a while? Right thinking may be difficult for many because most of us carry within us a huge burden of unbelief. Coping with this handicap may be our first priority. So let's look at our struggle with unbelief.

THE PRISON OF UNBELIEF

I read recently that a dime held at arm's length toward the sky covers 15 billion suns. We live in an immeasurable universe—yet this universe is just the pre-kindergarten for the new race of beings God is raising up. God's enterprise is so vast that an arena the size of our universe must have been essential to contain it. What is God trying to accomplish in His cosmos? God knows that life, which is given away returns to the giver in even greater vigor. Such life is self-generating and self-sustaining, and it is the only kind of life that is eternal by nature. God has actually invited humanity to participate in His kind of life. When I first heard this, something leaped within me, and I said, "That is the most extraordinary thing I ever heard and I want to be part of it." Why wouldn't anyone? For those who don't choose it, isn't it because another kind of life has already taken root deeply within them and it is unwilling to give itself up? And yet, doesn't that kind of life diminish and cripple those who are caught by it and cling to it?

Plus, we have an adversary, who is committed to capturing our hearts and minds and controlling us from within. Don Quixote, the mad knight, in the motion picture, "Man of La Mancha," did battle with both imaginary and real adversaries. He was successful in his battles with imaginary adversaries, but he was undone in his battle with the real adversary, the great enchanter. The great enchanter hovers over us and chants his lies. He tells us that we are damaged goods. He whispers, "You can't," when we can. He whispers, "You won't," when we could. He says, "You are not," when we are. The great enchanter holds his mirrors before us and shouts, "Look, Look, Don Quixote," and when we look into his mirrors, we see what he wants us to see—a mad knight. So we are encouraged in our unbelief by a powerful adversary who wants us to remain in the prison of unbelief.

Paul says, "…We are not fighting against people made of flesh and blood, but against persons without bodies—the evil rulers of the unseen world, those mighty satanic beings and great evil princes of darkness who rule this world; and against huge numbers of wicked spirits in the spirit world" (Ephesians 6:12). How can we prevail against such odds? We could look into another's mirror. What will we see when we look into God's mirror? We will see one made in God's image, a never-to-be-duplicated masterpiece, and one created to live life as God lives it. We will see all the ingredients in place to become another son or daughter of God. But, only if we look into God's mirror.

When we look at Jesus, we see one who recognized magnificence in us. He saw such greatness in us that He was willing to forsake His own life for our spiritual awakening. Who is telling the truth and who is telling the lie? I would hesitate to argue that Jesus is the liar.

We are already broken and in need of repair when we first hear of the greater way. So, isn't it true that in order to participate in the greater kind of life, one is required to go on a voyage, (journey or pilgrimage) in pursuit of it?

The prophet Habakkuk asked the question, "Must I forever see this sin and sadness all around me"(Habakkuk 1:2)? His question was answered, "But these things I plan won't happen right away. Slowly, steadily, surely, the time approaches when the vision will be fulfilled. If it seems slow, do not despair, for these things will surely come to pass. Just be patient! They will not be overdue a single day" (Habakkuk 2:3). Habakkuk spotlights a reason that creates reluctance to go on this voyage. We have so far to go, and fulfillment may be delayed. We have been invited into partnership with God to bring the cosmos into order and fulfillment, but we are so broken that we cannot believe in such a destiny—much less begin to move toward such magnificence. The job of getting us from where we are to the place where we need to be is so big that we fear we cannot take such a giant leap. We are frozen by our own unbelief and are unwilling to begin a voyage that may take more than this lifetime.

Also, we are conditioned to think that something too good to be true is not true. Can it be true that the champion of the power of love demonstrates His character by laying down His life as it has been and chooses to live for us instead of for Himself? His life is so given that it returns greater rewards than the cost of it and God becomes greater than He was before, and He astounds us by offering this same quality of life to us. Could this be true? Yes, it is true. Biblical evidence declares it. We should come to believe it or forsake biblical integrity.

Some readers may find the idea of an expanding God hard to comprehend. Eternal life cannot be measured in time, for there will be a place where time ceases. Eternal life may better be measured by its nature, not by the length of its years. Forever expanding, rather than forever existing, is possibly the best definition for eternal life.

We have difficulty believing that God has invited us to participate in the same quality of life He embraces. What will it take to break us out of this prison of unbelief? Two things will be helpful: 1). Beginning to understand God and 2). Beginning to understand the nature of the voyage.

BEGINNING TO UNDERSTAND GOD

We will never completely comprehend God, for our minds cannot be stretched enough to encompass such a Being. He will inevitably be more than our minds can grasp, but we can begin to see and understand Him. How will we be able to accomplish this? Jesus told Nicodemus that something happens inside people who look (focus) upon Him (John 3:14-15). When we focus upon Jesus, we see Him sacrificing His life in order for us to have His kind of life. Jesus is the mirrored image of the Godhead. So, we see God the Father, God the Son, and God the Holy Spirit investing their lives in us. Their destiny has been interwoven with ours. This means that, if they cannot accomplish their enterprise, their destiny is bound to ours, and their dreams and expectations for their own futures are altered. And we see God signing such an agreement in blood. Unbelievable, isn't it, but will not an honest examination of Jesus reveal that all of this is true?

Those who focus upon Jesus see in Him the kind of life that permeates the Godhead. They see God agreeing to prove the superiority of His life by loving and serving us until we are convinced of His superiority and we voluntarily submit to His sovereignty and authority, gladly choosing to pursue His kind of life. Will such a God as this capture our imaginations and draw us into a spiritual pilgrimage? If this does not capture our imaginations, is there anything else that God can do? Has God spent His strength in doing all that He can do? Creath Davis says, "Beyond this God cannot go."[5] It seems true that failure to recognize the beauty in what the Godhead has done will leave us with un-captivated imaginations and bind us in self-destructiveness and self-centeredness forever. Failing here, there is no other power in the cosmos that can rescue us.

Beginning to understand God, then, can draw us into a voyage toward a magnificent destiny. We are also drawn into the voyage when we begin to understand the nature of the journey.

BEGINNING TO UNDERSTAND THE NATURE OF OUR VOYAGE

Second, we begin to see and understand the nature of the voyage. It is a pilgrimage that has no end. We can see the path until it disappears over a horizon, but beyond that we cannot tell where it goes. We are voyaging toward God's kind of life. God loves and serves, then the returns from such life expand instead of diminish His own being. God becomes greater than He was before, enabling him to love and serve even in greater expanse, and again the returns expand His being. Does such life have an end? No! The sky is not a limit to where such life can go. God's kind of life is *ad infinitum,* and we are voyaging toward this same quality of life.

Spiritual voyages are not like physical voyages where you take steps in succession. We will be disappointed if we expect step-by-step instructions. The spiritual voyage is not like walking one step at a time along a path; it is more like being enticed into a boat and being carried by a stream, which ultimately transports us to a new destination far away from

---

5   Creath Davis, *Beyond This God Cannot Go* (Zondervan Publishing House, Grand Rapids, Michigan), Cover.

where we embarked. Spiritual voyages have a beginning, but there comes a place where something takes control of us and carries us where we alone cannot go. Some define the voyage as getting on a toboggan that travels its own speed and direction. Others define the voyage as getting on a roller coaster that has no throttle, steering wheel, or brakes and terrifies its riders.

We have been invited on a voyage that leads to God's kind of life. It frightens us to dream of such magnificence. Do we dare aspire to such greatness? Or, will we shortchange ourselves unless we do? Nelson Mandela has said:

> "Our deepest fear is not that we are inadequate. Our deepest fear is that we are powerful beyond measure. It is our light, not our darkness that most frightens us. We ask ourselves, who am I to be brilliant, gorgeous, talented, and fabulous? Actually, who are you not to be? You are a child of God. Your playing small doesn't help the world. There's nothing enlightening about shrinking down so someone won't feel insecure around you. We were born to make manifest the glory of God that is within us. It's not just in some of us; it's in everyone. And, as we let our own light shine, we unconsciously give others permission to do the same. As we are liberated from our own fear, our presence automatically liberates others."[6]

---

6   Marianne Williamson, *A Return to Love* (Harper Collins Publishers, Inc. 1992), (quoted by Nelson Mandela in his inauguration speech in 1994).

This is not a license for egomania. It is a challenge to release all the image of God that resides within us. Isn't it all right to love ourselves if we love the right self?

Is our image of God too small? We have difficulty-seeing God making messiah like children out of ordinary human stuff. This is just too impossible for God, as we view him. But, what if God is greater than we imagined? What if God's love really does prompt Him to sacrifice Himself in service to humanity, raising them up to be partners in the government of the cosmos? And, what if God is doing the unexpected—capturing the hearts of wayward persons and reprogramming them for the God kind of life? If such a God exists, don't we need to give Him our undivided attention? And, when we really focus, won't we see that what we've been saying here is true?

The ultimate triumph of God belongs to His family as well, for He has bound His triumph to their fulfillment. We are broken, frozen, and the voyage terrifies us; yet some who follow Jesus will be enticed upon it. God has vowed to see His family through the voyage, and He will not have succeeded in His enterprise until our destinies have been fulfilled. I will attempt to share with you the voyage as far as I can see it.

CHAPTER 3

CAPTIVATED BY THE CHARACTER OF GOD

> "His unchanging plan has always been to adopt us into his own family by sending Jesus Christ to die for us. And he did this because he wanted to."
> (Ephesians 1:5)!

Our actions tell the world who we are and the acts of God tell us who God is. When we discover the character of God, an aura will surround us, for we will be captivated by what we see. Our captivation by the character of God presented in this chapter is the single most transforming occurrence in life. We sit like ready rockets upon our launching pads waiting for a button to be pushed to ignite us into propulsion. The capturing of our imaginations will ignite us. Upon ignition, adinfinitum (eternal) life is initiated; life where there is never a saturation point, life without diminishing returns, life where there is always the best is yet to be. Grace can draw us into such exuberant lives. Those who miss this, miss the purpose for living. Is there an act of God that reveals God's grace and tells us who God is? Yes, God showed us what He is like when he adopted us into His family.

ADOPTED INTO GOD'S FAMILY

What does it mean to be adopted into God's own family? For many, it is intellectual assent to certain biblical precepts and consent to involvement in religious entities such as church membership, Bible study, and worship. The above scenario only results in one taking hold of something. It all comes under our initiation, our discretion, and our control. Churches constituted of such members may be an embarrassment to themselves and all Christians. These members may become either anemic Christians or pseudo Christians who do not demonstrate vital Christianity.

What has been left out of the above formula? Is the deal done when one consents to certain biblical precepts and involves him or her self in religious entities such as church membership, Bible study, and worship or, is the deal done when the character of God revealed in His Son, Jesus, captivates our imaginations? Jesus is the Word of God expressing the character of God in human form. Anyone who wants to know what God is like can examine Jesus. The first disciples were drawn to follow Jesus, and in following him they saw, touched, and heard about God's kind of life. What they saw took hold of them and would not let them go. But, not all of them and not quickly for any of them!

At least three classes of people are drawn to Jesus: the seeking, the curious, and the status seekers. None of these begin their journeys captivated by the character of God. The seekers may have the best shot, but even status seekers may become captivated by what they see, touch, and hear. Judas may have been a status seeker, but he never saw the picture. Yet, James and John may have been status seekers too, and they were ultimately caught by the kind of life they saw in Jesus. Nicodemus, who came to Jesus during the night, was curious, and his curiosity may have led to his captivation. Peter was a hungry seeker who had become nauseated with anemic religion. Peter may have been the first to be captivated by what he saw.

Not all who are attracted to Jesus become citizens of the Kingdom of God. Judas was not only attracted to Jesus but he was a key player among the disciples. Judas was the treasurer for their fellowship. Churches need to be aware that just any response to Jesus is not sufficient. Beginning relationships may fall short of followers being caught up in the life and purposes of the kingdom. If those relationships do not ultimately lead to a captivation by God's kind of life, there appears to be something wrong in their relationship.

It is not my intention to inject guilt where guilt is not necessary, but followers of Jesus can examine their relationship with Him and possibly be enticed toward richer life. The question is not, "What brings us to Jesus;" the question is, "Where does our relationship with Jesus lead us?" Shouldn't our relationship to Him lead toward captivation by the character of God? For, God's ultimate triumph awaits the captivation of His family.

CAPTIVATED

What is it about the character of God that should captivate us? A science fiction movie plots an alien invasion in which beings from another planet take over the lives and bodies of earth people to accomplish their own designs upon earth. The writer of that script captures the predicament of all humanity. Another kind of life seizes our beings for its own purposes, and we do not even know it. When we understand humanity's Sin problem, it makes us ask, "Why does God want to mess with us?" Yet, God has a keen interest in us and He has taken drastic measures to rescue us. This should at least get our attention, and when God has our attention, we may be captivated by something bigger than ourselves, and what might that be?

THE PLAN OF THE AGES

Paul suggests that understanding God's plan of the ages will captivate us when he states, "His unchanging plan has always been to adopt us into his own family by sending Jesus Christ to die for us. And he did this because he wanted to" (Ephesians 1:5)! The last sentence in this verse tells us that God did this because His nature compelled Him to do it. Does this act of God tell us something about His character? Yes!

The triune Godhead; Father, Son and Holy Spirit have a master plan, and couched within that master plan is what Christians proclaim as the Christian worldview. That view encompasses the idea that a basic flaw erupted in the heavenly realm; God's preferred quality of life was challenged by an interloping quality of life. Such a crisis necessitated the formulation of the plan. The formation of the universe was the initiation of that master plan, for this would provide a temporal realm where the issue could be resolved without shattering the eternal realm. So, the purpose of the universe is to be the arena where the issue of whose life is supreme will be resolved.

God's preferred quality of life is to love and serve, laying Himself down in preference to the fulfillment of others, knowing that giving Himself to others is the only way to be eternally expanded. Adversely, the interloping quality of life prefers to be independent from all others—serving him first, which automatically leads to consuming others and requires the adversary to use power and control to maintain his self-preservation. Therefore, the only possible conclusion to adversarial life is chaos and ultimate destruction of all, for when all have been consumed the adversary no longer has a source to sustain himself. Satan (Lucifer) is destined to lose.

What is God doing within His family that will be the proof of the superiority of His position? He is raising a family, a holy nation, or a new race, which will be faultless, and He is doing this with broken and wayward free spirits. No wonder God's adversary thought God to be mad—yet when God pulls this off, there will be no doubt about whose kind of life is supreme.

IS THE PLAN WORKING?

How well is this plan working? The world at large is mostly unaware of God's master plan, and few of those who are aware have been moved into faultlessness or captivation. Does this mean that God made a mistake?

Assume for a moment that God knew beforehand that progress was going to be slow and assume that God knew the plan would be costly, anguishing the divine Godhead. Remember God's answer to Habakkuk, "Slowly, steadily, surely, the time approaches when the vision will be fulfilled just be patient! They will not be overdue a single day" (Habakkuk 2:3 b)! In order for God to back away from this plan, He would have to betray His nature and declare invalid the quality of life He saw as supreme. This would be a betrayal of Himself and God can be counted upon never to do this. Will God's plan work? God knows it will, and when we know it too, we will be captivated by something larger than our selves.

What God is doing in humanity is for His own glory, but are we aware of the great privilege that has been extended to us? God has exposed His character in the Christ and that character has the capability to captivate us and carry us upon an impossible journey. That journey has no end, for we are journeying toward the kind of life that has no end. We are reaching for comprehension of a being that is incomprehensible. Then why reach for understanding? Because, the more we understand, the more captivated we become and the more this kind of life inhabits our beings.

WHAT IS THE IMPACT OF CAPTIVATION UPON US?

It is our captivation that mends our fractured hearts. The flaw in humanity is a corrupted control center, (heart). Altering our control centers is something that we are incapable of doing, for our control centers drive us, controlling us from within. Our control centers are animated by the values held therein. We belong to whoever implants their values within us, for we are value-pursuing beings, not rational beings. We use our rationale to invent reasons for doing what our values compel us to want to do.

God's adversary, who is compelled by his selected nature to use power and control tactics, has seized our control centers for his purposes. He has cleverly infused His values within our control centers, (hearts). Therefore, we do not belong to ourselves; we belong to him. We are driven by an alien kind of life that seized control of us. We are driven by the kind of life that deifies itself. Is there anything that we can do to liberate ourselves, but look to Jesus? Boris Pasternak dramatizes the arrival of Jesus upon the world scene in his classic novel, *Doctor Zhivago* (The motion picture omits this quote):

> "Rome was a flea market of borrowed gods and conquered peoples, a bargain basement on two floors, earth and heaven, a mass of filth convoluted in triple knot as in an intestinal obstruction There were more people in the world than there has ever been since, all crammed into the passages of the Coliseum, and all wretched.
>
> And then, into this tasteless heap of gold and marble, He came. Light and clothed in an aura emphatically human, deliberately provincial, Galilean, and at that moment gods and nations ceased to be and man came into being-man the carpenter, man the plowman, man the shepherd with his flock of sheep at sunset, man who does not sound in the least proud, man thankfully celebrated in all the cradle songs of mothers and in all the picture galleries the world over."[7]

It would first appear that we who are caught frozen in Satan's grip of worthless values are hopelessly doomed. But there is hope. Jesus invaded our misery, and now there is evidence of a cure. We revel in the realization that as long as one heart feels His tug toward new life, He who has come to capture our hearts and carry us where we alone cannot go has not yet lost.

In looking upon Jesus, we are captivated by what we find and new values are implanted within our control centers. In

---

7 Boris Pasternak, *Doctor Zhivago* (New York: Pantheon Books, Inc., 1958), p43.

examining Jesus, we discover one who decided to become one of us forever. Whatever He was or could have been was forever forfeited in preference to becoming the head of God's household. The cross was a physical demonstration of this laying down of life, which was decided upon before the foundations of the world were laid. Jesus has demonstrated for us the kind of life that permeates the Godhead. When we see God's character, there is a response in our control centers that are at the core (heart) of our beings.

Jesus enters into relationship with us for the purpose of altering the control centers of our beings; not because He wants to lord over us, but because He wants the automatic pilot of our beings to be positioned and programmed properly. Paul calls our captivation a kindness and a favor (Ephesians 1:6 and 2:4-5), and it is, for such captivation leads us to a glorious destiny. We don't have to be afraid of God. God is not out to get us—He is for us. The behavior of God revealed in the plan of the ages shows a God who can be trusted to put our best interest first. We do not have to be afraid to examine the power of God's love, even though it will captivate us. None of us are self-animated. We have never been self-driven. We are either under the power and control wielded by Satan or captivated by the power of God's love expressed in Christ. It is a myth to assume that one can be self-animated. Those who pursue it all their lives will die without it. But freedom is readily available for all those who come under the influence of God's love and experience a heart change. And when the hierarchy of our core values is rearranged, we can be trusted to perform correctly, if given freedom, and this is exactly what God does when His children are captivated by His love.

C.S. Lewis has noted that whenever we place a lower value above a higher value, we loose both. The core values of all humanity have been tossed topsy-turvy. We will never function correctly until our heart (core) problem is resolved. In following Jesus we are made aware of and captivated by the character of God. When God is given His rightful place in our system of values, other values fall into their rightful places. With a healed core, we can be trusted with freedom, and that is exactly what God does for His family.

FREEDOM TO GO WHERE AND DO WHAT

Does the captivation of our core by the magnitude and beauty of God's kind of life, which has been fleshed out for us in the Christ, have a predictable course? Yes, Cosmic Warriors, such as Paul, become the willing servants of Christ. Could this be the reason why many avoid captivation? We intuitively know that our captivation leads to servant life and stressful situations, like Paul's imprisonment, and avoid it. The drive for self-preservation is the strongest drive in human personality. Therefore, avoidance of stress (pain) is a high motive upon our agendas. So, we establish safe zones, which we are unwilling to depart. Knowing that passion (captivation) could draw us out of our safe zones prompts us to avoid passion. But such avoidance introduces us to its own kind of stress. Living without passion interrupts all our human relationships, for we find ourselves in unloving conflict with those we should love, like parents, siblings, extended family members, spouse, children and grandchildren, neighbors, fellow churchmen, employer, employees, clients, the poor, the disenfranchised, our enemies, and on and on.

Is the avoidance of stress (pain) an option in this world? No! Our option is the kind of stress we choose to live under. There is stress that comes from being captivated by the character of God, which stretches us. And there is stress that comes from broken and unfulfilled relationships, which diminishes us. Do we want to live under the stress that comes from loving or do we want to live under the stress that comes from not loving? We are at liberty to make our choice, but God knows what that ultimate choice will be for all who are captivated by His character. And those who are on the voyage, even though unable to make the correct choice now, will eventually make the right choice.

A captivated core takes us where it wants to go. Then why is there such a delay between coming under the spell of God's loving kind of life and spending our lives to love and help others? It is because our captivation is not yet complete. Are the level of our captivation and the level of our servant life inseparably linked? If the answer is, "yes", then we have a dependable thermometer to measure the extent of our captivation. Those who will be honest about the extent of their servant life will know the level of their captivation. In most instances they will not have to drum up repentance, it will explode spontaneously.

The character of God has the potency to captivate us by its own power. We do not have to captivate ourselves. This is something that is not going to occur because we do a lot of spiritual grunting and groaning. But it is something that will occur to those focusing upon Jesus. Captivation does not require our faith. When captivation occurs, our faith will explode. For trust and belief is not our work, it is God's work in us. The character of God revealed in Jesus will captivate our imaginations and carry us upon a journey that transforms us into people who become God's family, reflecting much of the same kind of life that is in the Godhead. Remember Jesus' admonition to Nicodemus, all that we need to do is to look upon Jesus (John 3:14-15).

Captivation by the character of God has resulted in the emergence of Cosmic Warriors throughout Christian history. It still results in the emergence of Cosmic Warriors. So, captivation is part of the stream that carries those on the journey toward becoming God's family who win His case for Him. God will consider Himself triumphant, when this stream has transported His family to their fulfillment.

CHAPTER 4

SPIRITUAL BANKRUPTCY

> "It is a broken spirit you want—remorse and penitence. A broken and contrite heart, O God, you will not ignore."
> -- Psalm 51:17

The images we hold of ourselves greatly determine who we become and how we behave. This is why churches and other institutions treating people as numbers (objects), instead of as persons, causes so much damage. Such treatment is a form of murder that kills the sensitive human spirit and causes people to behave more like objects than persons. The loss of personhood strongly impacts a culture, causing people to perform miserably. It is possible for churches, family units, social services, healing institutions, care facilities and educational institutions to treat people as objects for their purposes. The end results become abhorrent behavior. Spiritual bankruptcy may make us aware of our role in producing cultural decay. This is something that we do not want to see in ourselves, yet seeing our bankruptcy can lead to awakening us to reality, which is the only feasible starting place for growth in understanding.

Spiritual bankruptcy is a dreaded venture, for many are already looking down upon themselves, and spiritual bankruptcy places us under additional siege. But, spiritual bankruptcy is a necessary venture for those embarked upon a spiritual voyage. In spiritual bankruptcy we discover our true self, which is both broken and magnificent. The experiences of Jacob illustrate these realities.

* * * * *

The midwives who attended Jacob's birth observed the second-born twin holding the heel of the first-born so they named him, 'Jacob'. In Hebrew 'Jacob' means 'Grabber.' This became the image Jacob held of himself, and he lived up to it. He grabbed his older brother's birthright and ultimately his blessing.

The broken relationship between Jacob and his brother, Esau, resulted in Jacob fleeing his homeland as a fugitive from his brother's wrath. He fled to the homeland of his mother's people where he continued to reflect the image he held of himself. He grabbed as much of his father-in-law's wealth as possible, thus becoming rich. His in-laws detested him, and his life was at risk because of their wrath. It seemed apparent to him and his new family that they should return to his homeland.

Imagine Jacob's spiritual state, running away from the wrath of his in-laws with nowhere to go but back toward the wrath of his brother. In this crunch Jacob was about to realize his brokenness. It was in this crisis and this spiritual state that God's messenger came to him. Jacob wrestled with the messenger all night—then before daybreak he succumbed to the messenger and asked for his blessing. The blessing may have come as a surprise to Jacob, for the messenger asked him the question, "What is your name?" The question really was, "Who are you?" And Jacob's response really was, "I am a grabber." Jacob, squeezed by a crisis of his own making and enlightened by the recognition of his brokenness, was ready for a new understanding of himself.

The messenger told Jacob that he had the wrong image of himself and gave Jacob a new name, 'Israel', which means 'Prince of God.' This new name eventually brought to Jacob a new image of himself, a new nature, and new behavior.

* * * * *

Not only do we have depersonalizing institutions and unloving and uncaring people attacking and destroying our image of ourselves—we also have an adversary who seized control of us before we were born and infuses his warped values within us, values that diminish and cripple us. Add to this the dysfunctions, which exist in every home, plus the mess-ups we all commit, and you have a recipe for disaster. All humanity is broken, but spiritual bankruptcy is not just seeing the brokenness within—it is also seeing that we were made in God's image with potential to live life like God lives it. Therefore, we could all use a Jacob kind of experience to awaken us to both of these realities. There is a 'Prince of God' in every one of us.

I had a bad experience when I was eight years old. My mother and I were traveling from our rural home to Houston, Texas by train. The conductor was amusing himself, between local stops—interviewing me: "How old are you? What grade are you in? Do you have a girlfriend?" These were easy questions requiring only one-word answers. Then the conductor asked a more difficult question, one that required thought and verbalization: "What is your girlfriend like?" Embarrassed and at a loss for words, I blurted out, "Fat and juicy!" There was laughter from everyone in the passenger car.

The conductor laughed until his sides ached. My mother was embarrassed but laughed along with the others. This became a family story, told over and over with no one being aware that a sensitive boy's spirit was being smothered.

What do incidents like this do to a child? It made me feel like a 'goof up.' It drove me into a cocoon of safety, becoming a quiet recluse, feeling lonely, and afraid—resulting in nightmares and feeling that I would never be able to make it in life.

Brokenness is a proper place to embark upon a spiritual journey, for this is where we all are. Nelson Mandela's comment about the image of God being in everyone is true, but the image of God in us has been disrupted by a broken image of ourselves. We are all broken masterpieces of God. The truth is, none will ever embark upon a serious spiritual voyage unless they come to their own place of spiritual bankruptcy. Spiritual bankruptcy is not an enemy to be avoided; it is a friend to be desired. Just as discovery of his brokenness was a blessing to Jacob, it will be a blessing to us.

Like Jacob, there are some things we need to see about ourselves. We need what Hal Haralson in his book, *The Lost Saddle*, calls, "a cat scan of the soul." What will we see when we begin to discover ourselves? We may see that we have been deceived by our own dishonesty, divided by our disunity, and deadened by desensitization. But we will also see that we are deeply loved by God in spite of our brokenness and that we have unseen potential that often only He recognizes.

DECEIVED BY OUR DISHONESTY

Do we have difficulty examining ourselves because of our dishonesty? Dr. Nat Tracy would say to his classes, "If you can honestly look at yourself and not repent, you are free not to repent." By this he did not mean that anyone was really free from repenting but that honest self-examination would always lead to repentance.

Why are we dishonest with ourselves? We do not want our brokenness to be known, so what do we do? We hide it behind a mask of acceptability. However, if we are not careful, the brokenness we hide from others will be hidden even from ourselves. When that happens, we have entered into dangerous and destructive self-deception.

Some of this 'cover up' begins at church. When we become Christians, we want our lives to be consistent with the precepts of Christianity. We listen to the minister who calls for Christian behavior, and we imitate the Christian role models we have selected. We begin to behave like Christians, but we are only acting like Christians. The bruised spirit that prompts abnormal behavior is hidden behind the front of external conformity. We become like the Pharisees whom Jesus condemned for washing the outside of a cup but leaving the inside dirty.

When we delude ourselves, are we not in danger of losing our ability to respond from our hearts? Are we placing ourselves in the growing conditions for real life as long as we live a lie? Elton Trueblood says, "Realism is the only feasible starting point for advance."

DIVIDED BY OUR DISUNITY

Is there a separation between our heads and our hearts, thus dividing and crippling us? Repentance followed by growth would occur if we could see ourselves honestly, but it is difficult to honestly see ourselves because of our disunity. Satan uses a ploy to deceive us about ourselves. The Bible calls this ploy "double mindedness." James says in his book, "A double minded man is unstable in all his ways" (James 1:8, KJV). The separation of our mind from the core of our being (heart) creates a blind spot in our self-understanding, which allows us to be a different person in our core (heart) and see ourselves as entirely another person with our mind. For example—whenever we value anything material above the value we hold for God and His kind of life, we become idol worshipers. We are, in effect, practicing the same behavior as those who followed Baal, sacrificing their children and consorting with religious prostitutes. Obviously, our own deception is not as pathetic, but the principle is the same. Accordingly, we may allow petty material values to supersede the more real values in which we overlook the needs of our children for our own greedy or impure interests. We would not be able to do this without our becoming double minded, which creates a blind spot when we view ourselves.

Wholeness is one of the end results of having our heads and our hearts reunited. Such reuniting is a great personal victory. Whole people emanate an aura of light. They face life with the intelligence of their whole being. Jesus described such people as being the light of the world. They mystify their peers, for they demonstrate wisdom above and beyond their peers. Like Jesus, they become the truth laid beside the lie. Yet, they are like protective, hilltop cities drawing troubled people to themselves and to the God who loves, forgives, and safeguards all who come to Him for healing and real life.

The disciples demonstrated unexpected wisdom when they were in conflict with religious leaders and other officials. Their advantage in those circumstances could have been the reuniting of their heads with their hearts—giving them unusual wisdom. Will the Kingdom of God ever belong to people who are religious but double minded? No, it will belong to the people whose hearts have been melted by the love of God and whose new life springs from a core that has been made whole. The Kingdom of God belongs to people who have been made whole by having their heads and hearts reunited.

DEADENED BY OUR DESENSITIZATION

There is a degree of desensitization in all of us. Desensitization is a mercy mechanism that God places in creatures of prey. God did not want creatures of prey to be conscious of the horrible experience of being seized by predators. Desensitization relieves prey of the trauma of being torn apart alive and conscious. A sheep Shearer recognizes this mechanism in sheep. The Shearer will violently grasp a sheep by the wool upon its back, jerk the sheep upward off its feet, tilt the animal quickly with a push of his knee, and slam the sheep abruptly on the shearing floor on its side. The sheep immediately goes into a trance and is unmoving during the shearing process. It is totally oblivious to what is occurring. When the shearing is finished, the Shearer lifts the sheep to its feet, steadies it for a moment, and the sheep walks off, unaware that anything traumatic has happened to it.

This same mechanism exists in people who often become prey to horrible things that happen to us. We are incapable of dealing with such horror at the moment. These things numb and traumatize us, so we spontaneously desensitize ourselves to them. Desensitization is a gift from God, but it is not a proper way to continually live life. Desensitization is partial deadness, yet it is God's mercy sedating us to the horror that has happened in our lives. However, this means there can be a dark side in us that we have never seen, felt or dealt with. In our spiritual voyages we are too fragile to withstand a sudden enlightenment. To suddenly discover the dark side of ourselves could destroy us, so God lovingly allows us to take peeks through the door to our dark side and deal with lapses in character at a pace that will not devastate us. In love and understanding God allows us to make our spiritual pilgrimage within at a snail's pace. But should desensitization continue forever? No! Eventually the Cosmic Warrior needs to face the habitation of dragons living within.

Authentic Christians are on a voyage in which healing is being accomplished as we go. Therefore, should we sit in harsh judgment of other Christians who have not yet seen and dealt with all the darkness within—when neither have we? To jump upon others' unseen darkness can be a ploy to avoid dealing with our own brokenness.

SEEING OUR BROKENNESS ACCENTS THE LOVE OF GOD

Do you see what a mess God must deal with in order to have a family who will prove the superiority of His life? Awakening to this reality should produce awe and love for God who continues to strive with us even though we are unknowingly more wayward than we imagine.

When we allow ourselves to see the brokenness within us, we can begin to comprehend the love and forgiveness of God. This leads the serious spiritual venturer to come to an understanding of the unconditional love of God, the unconditional acceptance of God, and the unconditional forgiveness of God. Unconditional love is more than great love. Robert Williams, in his unpublished manuscript, says:

"In reality, it is the unconditional nature of God's love that bowls us over and eventually draws a response. The thing that melts away our arrogant posture is God's response to us when we abuse His love without cause… Could we abuse Him, outrage Him, crucify Him and He would still love us? Absolutely! Could we break every moral principle, become a rebel of His cause, distort the beauty of His character, become a criminal or prostitute, choose to be an infidel, and He would still love us? Emphatically! If there is any power in the universe that ought to shatter us right down to the core of our beings, it is this kind of love. The fact that God could and ought to retaliate, but does not, bowls us over!"[8]

Is there a way to overcome our dishonesty, double mindedness, and desensitization? Yes! The character of God is laced with love and forgiveness. When one begins to see the character of God, the need to be dishonest, double minded, and insensitive dissolves, for God already knows about us and loves us anyway. A light comes on within, and it will no longer be necessary to maintain our self-deception or desensitivity. When we know there is a cure, we will be able to see the warped values, attitudes, and character traits within us. This is excruciatingly painful, but at least we begin to see clearly.

A friend on the spiritual journey wrote, "I was so indicted by some of the messages that I had to stop reading at certain points, unable to sustain the angst of my own failures and despicable state. So great was my sensitivity

---

8   Robert A. Williams, Nat Tracy: Spiritual Genius, Chap. 8, *God's Unconditionalism*, (Unpublished Manuscript), tp.177-178.

to the commands, that I feared being lost forever, mired in my own selfness, with nowhere to turn. Claustrophobia beset me, but ultimately I couldn't turn away. The story of all our lives."

Is there a place where we can discover our real selves?

A PLACE OF SELF-DISCOVERY

Jacob's place of discovery was in the throes of crisis brought upon him by his brokenness. However, there was a supporting cast in his drama. He had the support of his loyal and loving wives, particularly Leah. Leah was the unwanted and unloved wife. Her father pawned her off on Jacob by tricking him, yet Leah became Jacob's soul partner. T.D. Jakes describes Leah when he states "Rachel had her beauty on her, but Leah had her beauty in her." Jacob did not realize what he had in Leah until later. But, upon his death bed, Jacob made his sons promise not to bury him in the country where they had immigrated, but to carry his body to their homeland and bury him in the same cave with his grandparents, Abraham and Sarah, his parents, Isaac and Rebecca and where he had buried Leah. We all need a place where we are embraced before we can make the awesome journey within and discover our brokenness. Where may such a place be found?

The early church practiced an intimacy of shared life that is seldom experienced in structured churches today. How did the authors of the Gospel accounts know about Peter's denial? We surmise that Peter admitted his shameful behavior to someone, perhaps to all his spiritual family. Why was it that Peter survived his shameful behavior and Judas did not survive his? We surmise that Judas held himself aloof from the family of disciples and never really belonged to that fellowship. In describing early church life, Findley Edge states;

> "The earliest churches met in homes of various Christians for fellowship, instruction, and simple worship. Eventually the church services followed a more definite pattern. In the first part of the service, inquirers were allowed to attend along with the 'faithful,' but at a certain point in the service the inquirers were required to leave and only the 'faithful' remained."[9]

Were those special times with the family of God for special purposes? They were probably times of intimate sharing, self-honesty, and self-exposure. It was a time and a place where they were embraced and loved in spite of brokenness. It was a place where the love of God became evident for them to see in their supporting community.

A common misinterpretation of such openness of life is to practice open confession of sins. Confession of sins can be dangerous, for in those confessions we often make known the sins of others without their knowledge or permission, which may damage relationships. We do not properly understand openness of life until we learn the difference between sins and Sin and practice confession of Sin. Our sins are those things we do because there is a problem in our core. It is this core problem, our Sin, that we expose, not the symptoms of it, which are already evident to all who observe our lives.

There is a place where confession of sins is helpful, but that place is not in open meetings or before numbers of people. Such intimate sharing needs to be in the presence of

---

9   Findley B. Edge, "A Quest for Vitality in Religion", (Nashville, Tenn.: Broadman Press, 1963), p.49.

one or two trusted proven people who have the integrity to contain confessions without spreading them around.

In the late sixties and the early seventies, our house church held worship services in outdoor camping areas for weekend campers. Our church members had become accustomed to sharing their lives openly with others. They followed this practice in the leadership of those outdoor services. After a rich sharing time in one of those outdoor worship services, an elderly man with a Methodist religious background commented, "This reminds me of services we once practiced in Methodist meetings. We called them unburdening services." Did early nineteenth century churches commonly practice openness of life? Would that be an explanation for the spiritual vitality evident in an age before our own?

The loving family of God is a greenhouse where spiritual bankruptcy can emerge. Spiritual bankruptcy is the fertile soil from which voyages germinate, spring forth, and Princes of God are born who will become Cosmic Warriors in this world and worlds to come. Spiritual Bankruptcy will result in the emergence of Cosmic Warriors who are relieved of swagger and strut, which nauseates many in the world, when they view anemic Christians.

It has been reported that Socrates said, "There are fools who think they are wise men. And there are wise men, which know they are fools. To know that one does not know is the beginning of wisdom." It may also be noted that there are sinners who think they are saints, and there are saints who know they are sinners. Sinners who think they are saints are occasion for great embarrassment to Christianity, but to know that one is a sinner is the beginning of authentic Christianity.

WHAT DID SPIRITUAL BANKRUPTCY DO FOR JACOB?

Not long after Jacob's wrestling match with God's messenger, Rachel died from complications while giving birth to Benjamin. The midwives came to tell Jacob that Rachel, his lovely wife, had died after the birth of their child. They also told Jacob that Rachel had named the baby, 'Benoni', meaning 'son of my sorrow'. Jacob refused to allow such a humiliating name to be given to his son. He insisted that the child be named 'Benjamin', meaning 'my right hand son.'

Years later, when Joseph brought his two sons to Jacob for a blessing, Jacob, now half blind, crossed his arms to put his right hand of strength upon the head of his younger grandchild, Ephraim. Joseph objected saying, "Father, you have your right hand of strength upon the younger boy." Jacob replied, "I know what I am doing." Jacob was not going to allow the same feelings of insecurity put upon him by midwives attending his birth to humiliate his son, Benjamin, and his grandson, Ephraim. He became a man whose sensitivity caused him to focus upon the feelings and well being of others. He became a proper patriarch, fathering the heads of the twelve tribes of Israel. Spiritual bankruptcy was the opening of a door to richer life for Jacob who finally lived up to his new name, 'Israel', which means 'Prince of God.' Will spiritual bankruptcy produce similar results for us? Absolutely!

Does God's grace prompt Him to make Himself vulnerable to His family? Does loving and forgiving them, while they are still broken, place God at risk? Yes! But, God does not fear that His enterprise will fail. It is we who fear it will. Seeing the love of God, who takes such risk for us, opens the door for us to honestly examine ourselves, for we recognize such love can cure any problem that we have. Then we are freed to become saints who know we are sinners. But the process undeniably confirms the reality that God's enterprise will not fail.

Isn't this what the Psalmist was saying when he wrote: "It is a broken spirit you want--remorse and penitence. A broken and contrite heart, O God, you will not ignore" (Psalms 51:17). Those who recognize their spiritual bankruptcy will become people who demonstrate real life. Therefore, spiritual bankruptcy is not to be avoided—it is to be desired, for spiritual bankruptcy is another element of the stream that carries us toward the destiny of becoming Cosmic Warriors who believe in and assure the ultimate triumph of God.

CHAPTER 5

LEARNING HOW GRACE OPERATES TO PUT AWAY SIN

> "Long ago, even before he made the world, God chose us to be his very own, through what Christ would do for us; he decided then to make us holy in his eyes, without a single fault--we who stand before him covered with his love."
> -- Ephesians 1:4

God is taking broken and wayward people and making sons and daughters of them—like His own Son. Why does God do this? He does this for Himself, for this is who God is. His being is saturated with the understanding and recognition that this is the only kind of life that can sustain itself eternally. What God is doing in humanity is for His own glory, but in doing this, a great privilege has been offered to us, and this is where grace impacts our beings. For the grace of God takes hold of our imaginations and transports us on what we might ordinarily deem an impossible journey.

Is learning how grace operates to put away our Sin an intellectual, academic exercise, or is it an experiential exercise?

It is an experiential exercise. God sees us as potential future partnership material, but we have difficulty seeing ourselves in such light. It could happen if we could believe it, but Sin has crippled us and sabotaged our belief mechanisms. Experiencing grace restores our belief mechanisms.

Perhaps this story will shed light upon the impact of grace upon our belief mechanisms.

* * * * *

After a class dismissal, I sat in the classroom with the professor and a few other class members. The life of Christ had been our study for most of a semester. Camaraderie had evolved in this class where there was mutual love, respect, and acceptance. The professor and others were mediating the love of God in the class. In this sanctuary I honestly examined my love for Christ and, with tears in my eyes, openly acknowledged, "I cannot love Him, even when I try!" Yet it was obvious that Christ's love for me was unwavering. This is experiencing God's grace.

My pronouncement was received in silence. The group sat in silent contemplation for a time then departed. A few days later, in private, one of the class members, a deeply spiritual young man, approached me and said, "I saw something beautiful in you the other day." What is beautiful about someone who acknowledges he cannot love Christ even when he tries? Such a person is spiritually bankrupt, honest and experiencing God's grace, and that is something beautiful.

* * * * *

The Apostle Paul prays that our hearts will be flooded with light so we can see something of the future that God has called us to share (Ephesians 1:18a). Does God see us as potential partnership material? Yes, biblical evidence declares that God actually sees people as His family who will be His primary agents in eternal enterprises.

In a 2007 basketball game between 25th ranked Texas Tech and 2nd ranked Kansas, Texas Tech won at home in double overtime by one point. A thunderous cheer erupted at the final horn. That cheer pales in comparison to the cheer in heaven when one wayward person responds to the grace of God, for all heaven recognizes where that one is headed.

Does God have a cure for our Sin, the twisted, broken nature that resides within us? Either He does, or there is no cure, for humanity certainly does not have one.

A CURE FOR OUR SIN

We deal mostly with the question, "How does God deal with our sins?" Sins (with a lower case s) are covered by God's love and forgiveness, and so is our Sin, but dealing with our Sin is a more delicate problem. Sin (with a capital S) is a corrupted heart (control center) whose nature has been fractured, and out of which flows our sins.

An aspect of the operation of grace in our lives is the mending of this broken nature, and it is done without destroying our delicate being. The power of God's grace does not overwhelm persons, making mindless robots of them. Mending our broken nature is a difficult task, so difficult, in fact, that God's re-creation of broken humanity exceeds His creation of the universe itself. How is this spiritual mending accomplished? It is accomplished by summoning in Christ the potency of the innocent suffering for the guilty. The writer of Hebrews says, "But no! He came once for all, at the end of the age, to put away the power of sin forever by dying for us" (Hebrews 9:26b).

We have heard for most of our lives that Christ came to put away our Sin. Yet, after all these years we are still living under its domain. Why? It could be that God chooses to let us squirm in our brokenness and ugliness long enough to be absolutely sure that we will never return to such life for all eternity. Also, it could be that we have yet to see and comprehend the magnitude of the sacrifice Christ has made. This results in our hearts being left un-impacted by the grace that can accomplish this transformation.

Will we ever be able to see and comprehend the sacrifice that has been made for us? Let's take another look at the sacrifice that should take away our Sin. The sacrifice of Christ may be viewed on two levels—the visible, physical sacrifice and the spiritual, more expensive sacrifice.

THE VISIBLE, PHYSICAL SACRIFICE

Some call this sacrifice of Christ on the cross "substitution on the lower level." This causes us to regret our sins, which made it necessary for Him to be there. Like the animal sacrifices that troubled and moved Hebrew children toward better behavior, it causes us to want to live better. Should we diminish the intensity and reality of this sacrifice? No! For the cross will not allow humanity to ignore the grace of God. While it demonstrates the rage of God against our sins, it also reflects His abounding love. Because of the cross, God can be intimate with sinners and never be accused of dealing with our sins lightly. The visible, physical sacrifice deals with our sins, but it is not a cure for our Sin, the crippled, broken, and twisted nature within us. The cross pictures a greater sacrifice that becomes the cure for our Sin. The cross gets our attention and directs us to look further and when we look deeper, we discover the greater sacrifice, which is almost an unbelievable reality.

THE GREATER SACRIFICE

The description below may shed some light on what the greater sacrifice entails. Perhaps a warning is in order—a Mother Teresa's type of life may lie in wait for those who comprehend the grace of God on a deeper level.

Some call the deeper sacrifice "substitution on the higher level." This sacrifice deals with our Sin, the crippled, broken, and twisted nature that controls us. Paul says, "The same one who came down is the one who went back up, that he might fill all things everywhere with himself, from the very lowest to the very highest" (Ephesians 4:10). This verse tells us that Jesus became the eternal Son. And His Father became the eternal Father of humanity, and Holy Spirit became humanity's eternal servant and companion. The Fatherhood of God, the brotherhood of God, and the servanthood of God became a reality because of all that the incarnation entailed. Holy Spirit and Father God did not abandon Jesus to go it alone in the redemptive enterprise.

Failure to see and understand the cost of humanity's redemption will result in cheapening the grace of God. Dietrich Bonhoeffer argued that it was cheap grace, failure to see the sacrifice of God on the deeper level that opened the door for Nazi Germany. Bonhoeffer argued that cheap grace allowed German Christians to comfortably sit in churches, doing nothing, while Hitler murdered six million Jews and countless disenfranchised members of their nation's community. Readers may note that Bonhoeffer was arrested, put in prison, and martyred because of his message.

In a study of grace, a class member commented, "There is no such thing as cheap grace." He was right; there is expensive grace, and there is highly expensive grace. Seeing only expensive grace allows us to remain un-captivated. But seeing God's highly expensive grace will capture our hearts and transform us into willing servants. Perhaps this is why we intuitively avoid allowing ourselves to see the greater sacrifice that God has made.

Risk for a moment examining highly expensive grace with me. Jesus' assumption of humanness is the highest compliment ever made to humanity. This does not lower Him to our level—it lifts some to His level. But note what Paul said; "The same one who came down is the one who went back up." This means the humanity that Jesus assumed in the Dessension, accompanied Him when He returned. He would forever live under the limitations of the humanity that He assumed in the Dessension. The nature of the Godhead did not change, but its direction was forever altered by the Incarnation. When Jesus permanently became a man, God the Father and God the Holy Spirit could not abandon humanity, for doing so would separate them from God the Son. This means that they attached their selves to all humanity and this means that they attached their destiny to ours forever. Their accomplishments would forever be limited by our accomplishments. They would now live in light of their commitment to us. They could never enjoy the luxury of an independent life again. Their delight would be in our achievements. They would sacrifice their lives so our existence could be elevated to life like theirs. This is the greatest expression of love and other-centeredness that the universe has ever witnessed and the greatest expression of love God has ever made. No wonder the angels rejoiced and sang at Jesus' birth.

Therefore, the suffering and sacrifice of the Godhead did not end in a few hours upon the cross or in thirty-three years between the birth and death of Jesus. God was not an avatar like the Greek gods, who descended into the world for an interval, then returned to their former status, unaffected by their brief interlude into the world. Christians often see only the death of Christ and fail to see the resurrection and the reality that the Godhead—Father, Son, and Holy Spirit now live solely to assure our fulfillment. This is the more expensive grace that captures our imaginations and draws us into inner transformation, which cleanses us of Sin, the twisted broken nature within us.

There is potency in the suffering of the innocent for the guilty. When God looked for a cure for our Sin, He reached for His grace—grace demonstrated for us to see in the innocent suffering for the guilty. If the real sacrifice of God demonstrated in Christ and participated in by the Godhead does not capture us and carry us on a journey toward new life, there is nothing left that God can do for us, for He has exhausted His strength, giving all that He can give. The Godhead has given to us their life and their all—if that does not grasp us, nothing else can.

Seeing the innocent suffering for the guilty can prompt a voluntary submission from within the guilty. A transition begins to occur in the depth of us. A new nature begins to awaken that is not characterized by self-love, but a new nature characterized by other-centeredness. And the beauty is—it is a life in which we delight. The grace of God, demonstrated in the suffering of the innocent for the guilty, is the only power in the universe that can accomplish such a transition. Such potency can re-create broken humanity and fashion a new creature to share in God's kind of life, lifting humanity to the kind of life God lives. In making such sacrifice, the Godhead was expanded. Therefore, we can never catch up with the Godhead—we can never be equal to them, but we can be like them in kind. God's kind of life ever expands upward and so can ours.

What will the sacrifice of the Godhead do for us? During a three-week trip to Africa in 1999, I heard Christians boisterously singing, accompanied by drums, a chorus in their tribal language, "We thank you, we thank you, we thank you, Lord. We praise you, we praise you, we praise you, Lord." Where did such understanding of and love for God come from?

My wife and I returned to Africa in 2002 as International Service Corps Missionaries. She assisted the Strategy Coordinator for all of Mozambique. I led in the construction of the first building of a Bible-training facility in Nampula, Mozambique. We also served together as volunteer coordinators for American volunteers coming for short-term special projects. I expected to encounter limited awareness of Jesus in Africa. Then my jobsite interpreter, Wilds, asked if he could gather neighborhood children under the cashew tree near the construction site for afternoon Bible study. I assured him that it would be fine. The next afternoon Wilds had 30 children gathered in the shade of the cashew tree singing choruses in Portuguese like, "Don't you know Jesus is good, don't you know Jesus is good, don't you know Jesus is good? Jesus is good. Yea! Yea! Yea!" Again, where did such understanding of and love for God come from?

David Livingston, a Scottish missionary and African explorer, became a trailblazer, mapping unknown inland African territories. He died upon his knees with his head upon his cot one thousand miles inland from Zanzibar. Livingston's prayer was: "May Heaven's rich blessings come down on every one, American, English or Turk, who will help heal the open sore of this world." Then missionaries began leaving Great Britain and America embarked on ocean steamers with a few personal possessions. When they arrived at some African port, they loaded their personal items into ox carts and headed inland, following maps charted by Livingston. Among those personal goods might be a head stone with their name and date of their birth carved upon it. They surmised that they might not return from the hardships of dysentery, malaria, bandits, or unknown diseases. Why did they go? They went because the grace of God, visible in the sacrifice of the Godhead's life for us, took hold of the broken nature within them and transformed them into people who could spend their lives for others—living life like God lives it. During my two trips to Africa in 1999 and 2002, I was witness to the fruit of those Missionaries' lives, for grace received became grace given, and the chain reaction can never be stopped.

When God's expensive grace impacts our hearts, we are captivated by something larger than ourselves and we begin to believe. With our belief mechanisms restored, we launch our journeys toward seemingly impossible dreams.

DREAMING SEEMINGLY IMPOSSIBLE DREAMS

God's plan is to forever settle the issue of whose kind of life is supreme. God will demonstrate the superiority of love and a servant life and blast the self-serving power and control kind of life out of the saddle. God will do this by loving wayward humanity, taking them and fashioning a new race of beings, who, when fulfilled, will win His case for him. God has reached into the grave and found the stuff from which will be fashioned His family, the new race, who will partner with Him in the government of eternity. Unbelievable, isn't it? His family's first assignment will be settling the issue of which kind of life is supreme. Such kindness amazes us, yet we cringe when we contemplate that God is pointing to us as evidence of what His love can do.

Can God pull off this deal? We may doubt it, but Satan does not. Satan was quite sure he had lost his case when he came to the third temptation of Jesus. He offered to abandon the world as the arena for settling the issue if Jesus would acknowledge some validity to his kind of life (worship him). Why would Satan do that? He did it because he was certain that he could never win in this world where the grace of God was being so dramatically displayed. Satan knew that he would eventually be defeated, if the contest stayed in this world. Jesus did not accept Satan's offer. Jesus' answer assured that the issue would be resolved in the world, not side stepped to be resolved at some later place and time. Satan is already defeated and he knows it! His nature prompts him to wreck as much havoc as he can in the time that remains—hoping that some miracle will turn his fate around.

When the self-sacrificing grace of God finally seeps into our hearts (the depth of our beings), we will understand and believe that God knows us, loves us, and wants us to be members of His family. Then the most potent force in the cosmos will impact us—God's expensive grace.

It had been a whirlwind life that stood His country upon its ear. He was called a bastard, a liar, Satan's imp, and accused of being anti-God. At a place called 'Skull hill' this young Cosmic Warrior was executed. If we had been there that day, we might have wondered, "What a waste of life!" Two thousand years have come and gone, and now He is the central figure of the human race. He unleashed the most potent force ever to impact the world—God's grace, grace that carries us on a seemingly impossible journey toward becoming the Cosmic Warriors whose Sin has been put away.

Grace to put away our Sin is an element of the stream that carries us toward becoming the Cosmic Warriors who will prove God's case for Him and pattern the world after heaven. Cosmic Warriors are the adventurers who will participate with God in the government of the cosmos, experience the kind of life that has no end, or saturation point, and live eternally with the expectation that the best is always yet to be. Learning how grace operates to put away our Sin will propel us to believe in the fulfillment of God's family, and accept the reality of God's ultimate triumph.

CHAPTER 6

SUBMITTING TO THE AUTHORITY OF GOD

"I will write my laws in their minds so that they will know what I want them to do without my even telling them, and these laws will be in their hearts so that they will want to obey them, and I will be their God and they shall be my people."
-- Hebrews 8:10b

Why do we hesitate to submit to the authority of God? The following story may show us the answer to that question.

* * * * *

A tall skinny boy, obviously from the country, was leaning on the fence near the ticket booth and loading platform for the roller coaster. He was experiencing his first fair. He watched with spellbound interest as youngsters boarded the cars, rode the slow climb up the first incline with their hands held high to show their courage, and then drop suddenly amid their screams and the roar of the trolley wheels on the track.

His vigil lasted for more than an hour. Once, he left his post and took three or four resolute steps toward the ticket booth, then stopped abruptly and returned to his former observation post. He was trying to work up the courage to take his first roller coaster ride.

It was almost an hour before he moved again. His decision came late. There was already a line at the booth. By the time he bought his ticket and moved through the turnstile, there was only one seat left—the back seat of the last car. If you have ever played 'pop the whip,' you know the effect of being at the end of violent and sudden motion changes.

He sat in the two-passenger seat alone and held his hands high above his head in an expression of naive courage. The cars climbed slowly to the top, seemed to balance briefly with the front cars over the top and the rear car near the top, and then plunged suddenly toward the bottom. The last car was jerked suddenly up as it completed the incline, then plunged down pulled by the weight and speed of the front cars. The 'sudden up' caught the country boy by surprise, for he was expecting 'down.' He reached for the handle bar in front of him, but before he could reach it the car plummeted down. There was daylight between the seat of his pants and the sides of the car. He must have caught the bar with the top of his toes or he would have been thrown completely out.

The front car was halfway up the next incline before the back car reached the bottom and slowed suddenly. The sudden slow down allowed the country boy to catch up with his seat. He resembled a cork driven into a bottle by a sharp slap of the palm.

The country boy was visible in the bottom of the car until it disappeared over the next incline. When the roller coaster came into view again, the rear seat appeared empty, but the roller coaster banked sharply into a turn, and the top was tilted so one could look partially down into the cars. The country boy was wedged tightly between his seat and the back of the seat in front of him where he remained until the end of the ride. When the cars came to a stop, he emerged from the floor of his car and walked shakily away without ever looking back, probably promising himself never to do that again.

* * * * *

We may possibly view submission to the authority of God like getting into a roller coaster. And it is somewhat like that, but submission is not a bad word and our submission to God is not bad for us. In fact, our submission to God leads to the richest life possible for us. Submission is assumed to be bad when it conjures up thoughts of someone lording over us. Whenever submission is forced, it is a bad experience. But God's submission to us was voluntary, and He will not force or require our submission to Him. However, failing to voluntarily respond in submission to God has its consequences—plus it may result in the loss of a relationship with God that is beneficial and rewarding. When submission is voluntary, it opens the door for extended unity between persons. Voluntary submission is to be desired, for it brings one to a closer relationship with God and a fresh approach to life.

My father tilled the soil on his farm with horses and mules. Those animals would often become unruly, kicking and fighting the harness, which required their submission. Such a fit usually resulted in getting the harness out of place, a leg over a trace-chain, a collar askew, a bridle over an ear, or some other mishap. With their harness in disarray, the task of pulling the plow or wagon became more difficult and self-injurious. Willing submission to the harness would have brought comfort and aid to the task assigned to them—but being dumb animals they could not recognize this.

Are we going to be like dumb animals that cannot learn that voluntary submission to God's authority becomes an aid to our lives? Isn't our acceptance of God's authority absolutely essential to living a fulfilled life? The writer of Hebrews says, "I will write my laws in their minds so that they will know what I want them to do without my even telling them, and these laws will be in their hearts so that they will want to obey them, and I will be their God and they shall be my people" (Hebrews 8:10b).

Where are we going to learn such valuable lessons so that God's laws may be written in our hearts? We can learn them in our early childhood home, in our marriage, in the crucible of life, and in our relationship with God.

LEARNING THAT SUBMISSION IS BEST FOR US IN OUR CHILDHOOD HOME

The fourth commandment states "Honor your father and mother, that you may have a long, good life in the land the Lord your God will give you" (Exodus 20:12). This is the first commandment with a promise—a long and good life. The principles (laws) that God has set forth are for our benefit, but we do not always recognize this. Learning to be submissive to the authority of our parents, even imperfect parents, prepares us for obedience to the principles that God has set forth even though we do not immediately recognize that these principles are beneficial. Learning submission to God's principles will prevent numerous instances of self-injury. The earlier we learn this, the better our lives will become.

Parents may make rules for their children purely for the sake of having the children do whatever they say. These become 'because I say so, rules.' God never makes 'because I say so, rules.' All of God's rules are for our benefit. Learning obedience to authority, even bad authority, equips children to become adults who are more likely to follow God's rules. Those children will grow into adults who avoid the pain of beating themselves up, battering their heads against the wall of God's rules.

Practicing obedience to parental authority prepares us to practice obedience to life-fulfilling principles. We do not come programmed with an understanding of life-fulfilling principles. So God's requirements may sound as if we are being asked to perform in a manner because God says so, but this is never the case.

An area where we often encounter conflict is in regard to sexual behavior. It is common to reason that spiritual principles regarding our sexual behavior are designed to prevent us from enjoying life. This is opposite of reality. The spiritual principle of fidelity to one's self and present or future partner is intended to enhance enjoyment, not to diminish it. When one breaks this principle, he or she is doing damage to himself or herself and their present or future partner. Does this sound like fun? No, it sounds like misery, yet countless individuals browbeat themselves in disobedience of principles, which were designed for their good. The amazing thing is that God is always present to bring healing of our brokenness and redirect us toward the most fulfilling life still available to us. Others, who observe the principle of fidelity, are rewarded with a lifetime of sexual enjoyment beyond imagination.

Young people that I counseled while serving, as Chaplain for the Texas Youth Council would contradict my council upon these matters saying, "Don't knock it until you try it." I countered with the argument that fidelity should not be knocked until one tried it. Any argument that can be used in defense of both positions cannot be a valid argument.

Children who learn submission to authority in their childhood home are blessed, but this does not exclude others, for God gives us additional opportunities to learn this lesson.

LEARNING THAT SUBMISSION IS BEST FOR US IN OUR MARRIAGE

The relationship between a husband and wife is like the relationship between Christ and His church. Jesus laid His life down in love and submission to the people of His church, fully believing that followers who love Him will reciprocate by voluntarily submitting to Him. Note that Christ first submitted himself to His church family. Then the expectation becomes that His church family will reciprocate by submitting their selves to Him. The church is His bride. Husbands should note that Christ first submitted himself to His bride expecting the bride to voluntarily submit to Him. This example confirms that husbands should first submit to their wives so the wife is motivated to submit herself to him. Mutual submission has always been a Biblical principle.

Husbands and wives who do not love and submit to each other will destroy each other. Yet husbands and wives who love and submit to each other may become partners with God in completing the re-creation of another person.

Do we lose anything in submission? In submitting to our marriage partner one must exit his or her cocoon of comfort and safety, which protects him or her from possible harm. There is risk here and that risk is real, but which is the greater risk—locked within our cocoon of safety or taking the chance that our submission will be reciprocated? Locking one's self into a cocoon of safety has disaster written all over it. Loving and submitting to our partners not only has the possibility of disaster, but it also has the possibility of great returns.

A husband and wife can aid in finishing God's creation, and they are the best chance in the world for this to occur. Men need courage to adventure—to go where no man has ever gone. Yet, in most men there is still a fearful boy who is afraid that he does not measure up. His destiny is in his wife's hands; she can nurture him or crush him. If she can love and submit to him, he is fortified with assurance that he is capable, and he will dream dreams and choose adventures big enough for the two of them.

Women also place their needs and destinies in their husband's hands. Women need to be nurturing and creative. In order for a wife to work her magic, she must have intimacy with her husband. Often a man's interpretation of intimacy is having sex, but most often a woman's interpretation of intimacy is having intimate conversations. So, in order for a husband to fulfill his wife's needs, he must submit to her need for her version of intimacy—that means giving himself and putting himself at risk, acknowledging the fears, guilt, hostilities, and feelings of inferiority that inhabit his inner being. Yet, where there are great risks there are possible great returns. If a husband can submit to his wife's need for intimacy, she can exercise her nurturing nature, fulfilling herself and her husband.

Husbands and wives have needs that can only be fulfilled by a response from the other. That response is the love and submission of each to the other. The message of unity in marriage is seldom responded to because it says what we do not want to hear. We do not like to hear that living at risk is the only way we will ever really live. We keep hoping that a loving God will change the rules for us, but that is exactly what a loving God will not do. It is not enough for two people to stay together, enduring each other; they must also submit to one another. Marriage is a test of authenticity and a training ground for learning a most valuable lesson in life; namely, that submission is a fulfilling way to live. Failure here has great consequences not only to our marriage, but we miss the opportunity to learn, on the human level, the valuable lesson that submitting to God also has its rewards. When husbands and wives love and submit to each other, they discover that submission is best for them, and they can then entertain the possibility of submitting to God's authority and reaping the fulfilling rewards that such life offers.

LEARNING THAT SUBMISSION IS BEST FOR US IN THE CRUCIBLE OF LIFE

I love the outdoors and am a skillful hunter. I gave this gift to God. My venture consisted of leasing ranches in Colorado and assisting hunters in their dream and goal of being successful in a big game hunt. The goal was also to serve landowners as well as hunters. Practicing proper wild game and land management was also beneficial for habitat and wildlife. Before God could utilize my gifts, I needed to learn how to submit myself to the authority of God.

I asked my wife if it would be all right for us to do this and she replied, "Yes, if you will allow me to go with you." Then, I asked God if it would be all right for me to enter upon such a venture. The answer that came was the same, "Yes, if you will allow me to go with you."

After being in this business for several years, I leased a new ranch before seeing it, but it was well recommended by people who knew about it. My family, along with several others from our church, spent two weeks on the ranch preparing the cabins and roads for the fall hunt. It was also essential to explore and become familiar with the habitat of this new, unexplored ranch.

In studying maps I saw a Rincon on part of the ranch. Rincons are glacier-formed. The ice that covered this region piled higher and higher until it began to slide to the south. In some topography and glacial conditions the valleys, filled with ice, pushed a depression into the north sides of the mountains, creating a deep hole. The valley ice spur would usually break off, and the glacier would slide southerly over the mountains. These deep depressions on the north side of mountains hold accumulations of winter snow, which melt slowly, allowing it to seep into the soil and create a moisture rich environment. Snow on the top, south, east, and west sides of the mountains is exposed to more direct sunlight, melts rapidly, and runs off before it can penetrate the soil—washing much of the rich topsoil away. A Rincon is ideal habitat for wildlife.

When I explored this Rincon, I made a remarkable discovery. Part of the valley spur had not broken away but had plowed a giant furrow up and over the mountain. This furrow furnished wildlife with a convenient access into and out of the Rincon. I had discovered the interstate highway into a hunter's dream.

My first inclination was to keep the place secret and enjoy it for my own pleasure. But as hunters arrived to hunt in the fall, I guided them to this place and gave it to them. Hunters were very successful there and extremely grateful for the experience of a good hunt.

Hardly knowing what I was doing, I was practicing submission to the principle of reciprocity. The principle of reciprocity guarantees that what we give away returns to us expanded. These hunters held me in high esteem. The esteem of these hunters was more enjoyable and productive in my life than success in a hunt would have been. Esteem from others should not be the goal of our lives, but the esteem (love) of others can be God's love mediated to us through them. I am not an ordinary coward—I am an extraordinary coward. I need affirmation, and these hunters provided the affirmation that I needed to venture where only the brave can go—like undertaking the writing of a book. When we learn that giving ourselves away is not costly, but returns the highest dividends, we have learned that submitting to God's authority returns the richest life available to us.

Practicing obedience to the principle of reciprocity taught me through experience that submitting to God's authority becomes a rewarding way to live. It was in the crucible of life that I learned this lesson. When we learn that God's authority is best for us and submit to it, a door opens itself to us. That door leads to exuberant, fulfilling, and joyous life.

LEARNING THAT SUBMISSION IS BEST FOR US IN OUR RELATIONSHIP WITH GOD

Submission to God's authority is absolutely essential to living a fulfilled life. If we miss that lesson in our childhood home, in our marriage, and in the crucible of life, we still have another chance to discover it. We can learn it in our relationship with God. Submission to God's authority is a difficult step, for we do not like to be under another's control, because they might take us where we do not want to go. When we are under God's authority, He is in control and we must go where He leads us—even if it is like getting into a roller coaster.

We mistakenly assume that if we resist the authority of God, we will remain under our own authority. We are deluded when we assume we can be self-animated. We are already under the control of God's adversary who is a champion of power and control. He has infused values within us that drive us from within, values that diminish us. We only think we are self-animated. When we reject the authority of God, we revert to another's control by default.

We can best place ourselves under God's authority when we recognize His right to be in authority. Even God has placed Himself under authority, the authority of His own character. He can be depended upon to always act in accordance with His chosen character. This provides the consistency that under girds the universe. God's submission to His character is an absolute upon which one may depend. Because God is under authority, He knows better than we do what it means to submit to authority.

Observe His Son in The Garden of Gethsemane. Jesus had submitted Himself to the authority of His Father and was pledged to demonstrate His Father's character. It is the Father's character to love the rebellious and try to save them. Therefore, Jesus could not abandon us for His own convenience. He had to fulfill His promise to demonstrate the character of God. Such love and submission earns the right to be in authority.

WHAT WILL SUBMISSION TO GOD'S AUTHORITY DO FOR US?

Living under the authority of God allows us to live by the principles God has selected as beneficial and woven into the fabric of our existence. These principles have been selected because they assure rich, full lives for us. God lovingly attached penalties for breaking these laws. Therefore, our rejection of God's authority has consequences upon ourselves. Those who resist the authority of God will shatter themselves upon the principles that under gird the universe, for when we break God's laws, we break ourselves upon them.

We did not create our world, God created it. We can only discover it and live within its laws as completely as we can. We may not like the law of gravity, for example, but it has its good purpose. If we ignore or rebel against it and step into an open elevator shaft, we will be hurt. In the same way, we cannot break God's principles without penalty. We need to learn that God's authority is best for us, accept it and live under it. For, submission to His authority is part of the current that carries us to our ultimate and highest destination.

Those who submit to the authority of God have discovered what a concert pianist knows. He knows that he does not have liberty to strike any note he desires. But he knows that submitting to the principles of rhythm and harmony gives him freedom to produce beautiful music. It is freedom, not liberty that we seek. Isn't that freedom available to all who will submit to the authority of God and become the Cosmic Warriors who overcome in this world and worlds to come?

Cosmic Warriors march to a distant drumbeat. They hold the keys to the kingdom of heaven. They will pattern the world after heaven, for they are the family that God is raising up to win His case for Him and to partner with Him in fulfilling the whole cosmic potential. When the cosmos is tamed and exhausted, it shall be folded up like an old coat and put away, but the family of God will venture beyond in realms unseen and untold for such realms are yet unmade and God's family may assist in designing and making them.

"What makes us think that we can escape if we are indifferent to this great salvation announced by the Lord Jesus himself, and passed on to us by those who heard him speak" (Hebrews 2:3)?

CHAPTER 7

COSMIC WARRIORS
IN THE WORLD

> "As you sent me into the world, I am
> sending them into the world."
> -- John 17:18

Jesus said to Peter, "And I will give you the keys of the
Kingdom of Heaven; whatever doors you lock on earth
shall be locked in heaven; and whatever doors you open
on earth shall be open in heaven" (Matthew 16:19)! Have
Christians been assigned the task of making a difference in
the world? Doesn't Jesus say that His followers will pattern
the world after the pattern of heaven? How will we ever be
able to accomplish such an assignment? The answer to these
questions may be found in discovering the impact of other-
centered servant life.

While in Africa, I visited and taught in a Bible Institute,
training prospective pastors and leaders of Mission Churches.
The instructor, Daipa Candeiro, a national church leader,
was teaching from Matthew's twenty-third chapter and
concentrating upon the passage which states; "The more

lowly your service to others, the greater you are. To be the greatest, be a servant" (Matthew 23:11).

He followed the reading of this scripture with this story: "In Africa a man and his wife walk together to work in a field. The man walks in front and the woman walks behind with an empty basket upon her head, two hoes in her hands, and a baby upon her back. They work in the field and return with the man walking in front and the woman walking behind with a basket full of potatoes upon her head, two hoes in her hands, and a baby upon her back." Then he asked a question, "Who is the greatest in Africa?"[10]

Elizabeth O'Connor wrote a book entitled, *Journey Inward, Journey Outward*. The thrust of this book is that our self-examination and the healing that follows will result in mission somewhere. The question that each of us may ponder is, "Where is my servant life to be?" The answer to that question is not difficult—the impact of our lives will be wherever we are. All of us are somewhere—in marriages, in families, at work, in businesses, or in churches, to name a few. These are some of the arenas into which Cosmic Warriors should advance.

IN MARRIAGE

If you are married, your marriage partner will be among the first to sense real life in you. There are few people in the world who observe us as closely as our mates—they will be the first to feel and see change in us. So our marriage is a frontier for advance and a primary place for our other-centered servant life to begin.

---

10   Daipa Candeiro, Nampula Bible Institute, Nampula, Mozambique, (Unpublished Class Story). 1999

Marriage is a great gift to us from God, for in marriage we may discover the absolute supremacy of other-centered life and the utter futility of self-centeredness. A vital marriage is the natural evolution of a married couple being relieved of self-serving interests. Self-centeredness promotes disunity instead of unity in marriage. Most of us who are married have felt the pain of an uncaring partner who could not see our need. Likewise, we have felt the exhilaration of being cared for when we were hurting. Let's examine the impact of other-centered husbands and other-centered wives.

Other-centered Husbands

The other-centered husband needs to learn how to nurture his wife's femininity. A special feminine characteristic is responsiveness, but before women can respond, there should be someone to whom they can respond. A man's self-interest should operate to help him choose godly life, for godliness reciprocates a responsive wife who makes her husband to be the center of her life. Pursuing godly character enables a husband to be a person to whom his wife can respond. He will do this for his wife's sake, and not merely for his sake. The man who refuses to make godliness the purpose of his life may diminish his wife's ability to respond. When she is robbed of this feminine quality, she may become cold and withdrawn, timid and fearful, or rival her husband's role as an initiator.

So, the other-centered husband needs to pursue and develop all of his manly characteristics. Again, this is more for his wife's sake than for his own. One godly, manly characteristic is aggressiveness, and a husband's aggression is more than sexual. Finding and pursuing worthy ventures for their lives is a symptom of healthy aggression. The man who ceases to be aggressive and adventurous cannot be an initiator and sentences himself and his wife to meaningless or mediocre lives. The passive husband binds the greatness that resides in him and his wife, for he has lost the manly qualities that prompt him to venture. If husbands will practice the principles above, they will discover that the servant life is enjoyable and rewarding, not tiresome or stressful.

Other-centered Wives

Other-centeredness in wives prompts them to nurture their husband's manliness. When a wife accepts her husband's aggression and nurtures it, she is rewarded with the security she cherishes, for his manliness is her security.

The man who has manly characteristics is an initiator. Men have a knack for beginning things and sometimes a reputation for never finishing them. Just as the wife is a responder, the husband is an initiator. As an initiator, he must be bold, aggressive, and adventurous. When a man chooses a wife, she is in custody of these manly attributes. It is in her power to nurture them or to kill them. In this way, a wife has the awesome power to make or break her husband's manliness.

How does a wife exercise her responsiveness to fulfill her role in marriage? A wife needs to respond to her husband's ideas and dreams. If she responds, "We can't do that," her husband is devastated, for what she has said to him is, "You can't do anything!" The fearful little boy, who still remains in many men, then rises to quench his initiative. As a creative nurturer, a wife is receptive of her husband's some times half-baked ideas, which in their origins can be incomplete. But under her responsive and creative feminine wisdom, a venture, which had no chance, becomes a practical, workable idea. The responsive wife excites her husband's mind into alertness, and his best thoughts are summoned. She responds appropriately to his ego needs, so he is relieved of his egocentricity, and his projects are not ego-centered but are founded in reality.

The roles of husband and wife may be seen in the stories of gallant knights and fair maidens. The knights rode forth gallantly in shining armor to conquer kingdoms, slay dragons, and rescue the oppressed. Maidens waited in the secure confines of their castles.

Young boys reading these stories probably see the knights going out. They seldom see them coming back, but if they do, they see them returning victoriously. Young girls reading these stories probably see the knights coming back, but they also see them returning triumphantly.

The real world is not always like that. A knight's real world was probably not like that either. Most likely, upon his return, his armor was battered and torn, his feather was singed, and his gallant steed was dirty and wounded. But, he came back to his castle and his maiden. Within himself, he was saying, "I'll never go back out there again." But he always did, for something good happens to men who retreat inside their castle walls defeated but under the nurturing care of other-centered wives.

Whenever a husband and wife discover the principles above and live by them, something beautiful emerges. The two of them become one, and their one life is greater than the combination of their separate lives. The husband becomes the expresser of their life. He knows that there is at least one person in whose eyes he will always be a winner no matter what happens. So, wherever he goes and whatever he does, she is with him. She intuitively knows this, and her natural drive for creativity is satisfied. She becomes very much like God, who at some point began to satisfy His relish for creativity through our accomplishments. Having found her niche, the other-centered wife is relieved of her restlessness and becomes secure in her role as an enabler.

A husband and wife who achieve this kind of life touch a divine reality—other-centered life enables the two of them to experience the power of unity. In marital unity, we taste the same quality of life that the Godhead found to be irresistible, for the unity of the Godhead must have been achieved when three beings chose to give themselves to each other.

IN BUSINESS AND VOCATION

Our world is progressing beyond the age when we were besieged by self-centered national imperialism. We now live in a world that is besieged by self-centered economic imperialism. Global economic interests have merged to form powerful conglomerates, which have the power to buy national leaders and their armies. Meanwhile small businesses have fallen like dominoes to the lie that self-serving business practices are the way smart business is done.

Cosmic Warriors have a challenging assignment. The first question we need to ask is, do we want the self-centered kind of life to prevail or do we want other-centered love-servanthood kind of life to prevail? If we prefer other-centered life and if we are faithful followers of Jesus, how should we face such formidable odds? Jesus served His world by being the truth laid beside the lies of His world. We can become the truth contrasting the world's presupposition that self-centeredness is the best way to survive. However, if we practice love-servanthood in our business, profession or vocation, we need to be aware of the fact that this kind of life seldom wins in the short term. Businesses following self-serving practices always win in the short term. But, businesses following love-servanthood always win in the long term.

Some congregations sing a hymn entitled, "Brighten the Corner Where You Are." The first stanza of this hymn says:

"Do not wait until some deed of greatness
you may do,
Do not wait to shed your light afar,
To the many duties ever near you now be true,
Brighten the corner where you are."[11]

It seems that, in my youth, we sang that song with more gusto than we sing it now. Will practicing the message in this song really work? Will one business in a sea of economic upheaval make a difference? Yes it can, for a rock tossed into a still pond sets in motion wave after wave until the entire pond is affected. Let's examine some principles whose practice might set in motion some waves that we would like to see in the business world.

Self-centeredness promotes distrust and fear between business and clientele and between labor and management. Each wants as much as they can get for as little as they can give. Self-centered people are incapable of doing much for each other without compensation. But, other-centeredness will allow one to practice the principle of giving more that they appear to receive. When we are limited by the amount that we can do only with reciprocation, little gets done, for there are no guarantees that others will respond appropriately to our efforts. In practice, giving more than one appears to receive has returns that may exceed those of self-centeredness. Doesn't the self-centered approach to business have imbedded within it the seed of its own destruction?

---

11 Words, Sir Robert Grant: Music, Francis Joseph Haydn; *The Modern Hymnal,* (Copyright 1926, by Robert H. Coleman, Dallas, Texas) p.324.

Should Cosmic Warriors confront this adversarial condition in order to change the way the world does business?

When people live by the other-centered-love-servanthood principle, real beauty and harmony emerge in business and labor-management relationships. Other-centeredness promotes feelings of faith and unity between would-be adversaries. Other-centered employees give themselves to their employer as if the business were their own. The concerns of management about the health of the business, the quality of the product, the availability of a market, production costs, and service to the customer become the concerns of other-centered-love-servanthood employees.

Other-centered managers treat their employees as their single most important resource. Their respect and concern for the individual employee is evident in all decisions and in all aspects of the business. The other-centered manager sees an employee as having the potential for growth and advancement regardless of how 'dead-end' the job may be. Imagine what it would be like to be associated with a company or business operating on other-centeredness and love-servanthood as the basis for its life. It would bring real excitement back into work.

The returns accrue spontaneously. Businesses, which take care of their customer base, see their customer base expanded, for customer loyalty is enhanced and demands for business services are increased.

Management taking care of their employees prompts labor appreciation, which is reciprocated by increased productivity, fewer hours lost to tardiness, absenteeism, and sick leave.

Employees who see their calling as doing the best job they are capable of doing regardless of compensation will increase company productivity and quality, creating a product or service that is in greater demand. Other-centeredness and love-servanthood in business and the workplace is a win-win proposition. The principle of giving more than we appear to receive really works. We will not be disappointed in the returns, for the returns will be greater than the cost. There may be isolated instances where the principle is short-circuited in the short term. But, in the long term this principle works. For it has within it the seed of its own expansion.

Why cannot people recognize that this principle works and act upon it? It is because another kind of life has seized control of us. We will only be free from self-centeredness when one greater than ourselves is liberated to transform our hearts and change us into different beings. Then we will be empowered to live different lives, take positions that place us in harm's way, travel a road less traveled, and shape our world rather than being shaped by it. We can become Cosmic Warriors, changing the way the world does business. We have already seen the power of such life in our world—it works.

IN OUR CHURCHES

Jesus responded to Peter, "And I say also unto thee, that thou art Peter, and upon this rock I will build my church; and the gates of hell shall not prevail against it. And I will give unto thee the keys of the kingdom of heaven: and whatsoever thou shalt bind on earth shall be bound in heaven: and whatsoever thou shalt loose on earth shall be loosed in heaven" (Matthew 16:18-19, KJV).

Will Cosmic Warriors flavor their churches with vitality and meaning? A personal friend, who is a former pastor and denominational leader, wrote:

"The western church is extremely dysfunctional spiritually and organizationally. It is passive, consumer driven, theologically and biblically shallow, and is not seriously and intentionally engaging in disciple making and the Great Commission. There are only a few pockets of renewal. Ministers are broken people and for the most part have not realized it because they buy into professionalism of ministry and become part and parcel to the dysfunctional nature of the western church. Thus, they expend tremendous energy and resources putting up fronts, developing a false persona, and meeting false expectations of sick parishioners. Consequently, the majority is empty, depressed, and wonder if there is any meaning or purpose to what they do. Or, they give up and just punch a time clock, with no hope of meaningful change in the church."[12]

If this appraisal is true, Cosmic Warriors should be realistic and expect controversy and conflict. If there is deadness in our churches and someone with real life is transplanted or resurrected therein, there will be inevitable conflict. For, being the truth laid beside a lie places us in harms way. This was the source of much of Jesus' conflict, for Jesus was the truth laid beside the lie of anemic religion.

Cosmic Warriors should not love conflict, but they should persist in spite of it. Conflict does not have to be destructive; it can be constructive. It can be the tension that draws a church toward better life. The courage to venture where conflict is inevitable comes from the assurance that

---

12   Don Fawcett, Personal Letter, (2008).

the church is indestructible (The gates of hell shall not prevail against it). If Cosmic Warriors' presence destroys a church, is this Jesus' church?

Cosmic Warriors may be battered and bruised, but conflict will not destroy them or the living church. They need to be careful and courteous, but conflict should not prevent them from bringing the life that is in them into their churches. Cosmic Warriors move carefully and slowly to bring their kind of life into their churches. They will accomplish this, not by their words or strength of their arguments, but by the power of their lives. Real life is contagious, and we can be confident that it will be caught by some of those who are exposed to it.

Should the Cosmic Warrior resort to the power and control tactics of God's adversary? No! They should always be motivated by love.

I met a retired minister whom I will call Duke. He related, "I was put out of a church when I was 55 years old. You are dead when you are put out of a church at that age." He had been pastor of a sizeable church where there were people who wanted a more spiritual ministry. They were tired of institutional deadness. They assumed that they had found some real life and did not feel supported by their pastor. So, they began a campaign to remove him. Duke was in another state examining the possibility of finding another church in which he could minister. While Duke was away, the restless members of his congregation succeeded in getting the church to enter into a business meeting. A motion was made to declare the pulpit vacant. There was open, hostile conflict; the meeting went on for hours, and some people left in disgust. When a vote was finally taken, the motion to declare the pulpit vacant was narrowly passed. Duke returned home to be told, "You have been put out as pastor of this church." It would be five years before Duke could find another place to minister.

Cosmic Warriors should not treat anyone as an object to be manipulated for their own benefit or comfort. Institutions, often without realizing it, treat people as objects, depersonalizing them and using them as grist for the institution's mill. This is personality murder, but putting Duke out of his pastorate was the same thing. We must be careful, or we may become guilty of exercising the same kind of life that we ordinarily would despise in others.

Everything Cosmic Warriors touch will be flavored by their lives. Their marriages, their business or vocations, and their churches will be impacted by who they are. Jesus describes them as the light of the world. Wherever they are will be an arena for advancement, and as they advance, the ultimate triumph of God moves closer upon the horizon.

CHAPTER 8

THE ULTIMATE TRIUMPH OF GOD

> "Oh, what a terrible predicament I'm in! Who will free me from my slavery to this deadly lower nature? Thank God! It has been done by Jesus Christ our Lord. He has set me free."
> -- Romans 7:24 and 25

Can we escape the strangle hold of power and control that Satan exercises over us and become believers who believe in the ultimate triumph of God who triumphs by the power of His love? Many do not believe it is possible and relegate any triumph of God and His family to a future realm outside this world or a return of Christ with a thunderbolt and a fist full of lightning bolts to enforce a kingdom of truth and righteousness with the power of His might. God's plan of the ages would have to be altered in order to maintain such a position. To assume such a futuristic stance entertains the idea that God's love was not great enough to get the job done here. Moreover, to prefer such a God who must alter His nature, abandon His love, and revert to power in order to straighten out the world, would also acknowledge His defeat instead of His triumph.

Nat Tracy, a mentor, instilled in me the hope of an overcoming church. Among his last words in my presence were, "I cannot understand why the church has not responded better." I had no answer then, but I do now. "It will!" Believers are, even now, being born and equipped through whom God will finish His creation. They know, even if it does not happen in their lifetime, their kind shall overcome. Remember Habakkuk's answer from God, "But these things I plan won't happen right away. Slowly, steadily, surely, the time approaches when the vision will be fulfilled. If it seems slow, do not despair, for these things will surely come to pass. Just be patient! They will not be overdue a single day" (Habakkuk 2:3).

Why do we doubt the ultimate triumph of God's love? It is because such a position takes us off the hook, which relieves us of the necessity of being anything or doing anything except waiting for our pie in the sky. Satan controls us by weakening our image of ourselves; therefore, we see all humanity as being incapable of God's kind of life. We see the enterprise of shaping such a race of beings too difficult even for God. But, is it—has our belief mechanism been irreparably shattered—or is there a way for our belief difficulties to be resolved? Paul states in Romans 7:24-25, "Oh, what a terrible predicament I'm in! Who will free me from my slavery to this deadly lower nature? Thank God! It has been done by Jesus Christ our Lord. He has set me free."

Remember what Jesus told Nicodemus? He said that if people would focus upon Him like the children of Israel focused upon the brass serpent, a new birth would occur (John 3:14-15). That new birth should carry with it a renewed belief mechanism. How does focusing upon Jesus accomplish this? Jesus comes into our lives and loves us with the God kind of love. We see Him forfeiting His right to an independent life and submitting Himself to loving and serving us for eternity. Eventually we get a different opinion of ourselves; namely, that we are important, for we are important to God. With our self-image intact and with a new image of God, our belief mechanism begins to be restored. Grace takes hold of us and carries us where we alone could not go. We begin to believe Jesus and John The Baptist, who said, "The kingdom of God is at hand (now)" (Matthew 3:2 and 10:7). This means that the kind of life we shall live in heaven can be entered into here. And, if we cannot live such life in total, we can at least begin to live it in part.

When our belief mechanism begins to be restored, we begin a voyage. It is a journey that has no end and along the way we will come to believe in what seems to be an impossible dream. It is the dream of a God who is etching His character into us. He will accomplish this properly if it takes Him a million years. Then, we will become His family and His agents through whom He will act here and in eternity.

God is no fairy godmother who waves a magic wand to turn our rags into elegant gowns or pumpkins into coaches? Neither do mystic rituals cause us to believe or restore our belief mechanism. In our weakness we want sudden transitions without any involvement on our part, but God hammers us into shape in life's experiences.

What else is it going to take for our belief mechanism to be restored? Jesus said, "You will know the truth, and the truth will set you free" (John 8:32). When God's love and forgiveness frees us to see and know the truth about God, and ourselves, then we are freed to discover all truth, and the body of truth that one endorses can be expanded.

A mentor once said, "If the truth destroys God, let Him be destroyed." After recovering from my shock, I realized that the truth would never destroy God. It will positively confirm Him.

Try to imagine the body of truth as being like a giant pie with hundreds of individual pieces. Then imagine those pieces removed, scattered, and shuffled upon a large table. There may even be pieces from another pie upon the table. Imagine reassembling those pieces in the same body and exact position they originally held. Could it be accomplished? Yes, for each piece has intricate differences and similarities, which will only allow it to fit in its rightful place. Truth is like this, for all truth is interrelated and each real truth will be in exact compliance with other real truths. Trying to fit pieces where they do not belong will eventually reveal that they do not belong there. It may be part of the pie that came from another place or even another pie, and ultimately it must be rejected. An honest searcher for truth will eventually get it right. And, as the truth building progresses, it becomes more and more obvious where certain pieces fit. It is like the final stages of putting a picture puzzle together. The last pieces fall into their rightful places much faster because it is obvious where they fit and there are fewer pieces of the puzzle to sort through. Our body of truth is built similarly to this, and the sudden enlightenment that comes has been called, 'Seeing the light.'

Illustrations are usually simpler than the reality they illustrate. When we begin to assemble our body of truth, we are working with a mind that has already been crammed full of truths that only seem to fit. It is more difficult to unlearn than it is to learn. So, we are not only struggling to assemble the truth, we are struggling to decide which pieces of our body of accepted truth need to be discarded. Then we must replace the discarded pieces with pieces of the truth that fit.

God has given us a mind to use, and we should use it. Not using our minds is an affront to God. When our spirits are impure, our minds are crippled and untrustworthy, but when our spirits are pure, our minds become trustworthy. God's enterprise does not schedule the numbing of our minds; it schedules the awakening of our minds. Therefore, one does not have to be a rocket scientist, philosopher or a theologian to master truth. We only need to become an honest searcher for the truth and use the minds that God has given us to sort out the truth. This process is highly accelerated when spiritual growth and maturity seeps into our hearts and makes them pure.

So, how can we come to believe in the ultimate triumph of God? The body of truth, which we endorse, can reconstruct our belief in God's ultimate triumph. The reconstruction of that which we hold as true is usually a long journey. It usually does not happen overnight, but it can happen.

Here are some of the individual truths one may need to deeply believe before they can believe in the ultimate triumph of God:

1. Three beings bound themselves together in unity, becoming one, and formed an undefeatable coalition, which we see and call 'The Triune Godhead.'

2. The Godhead recognizes and embraces the eternal kind of life—life that is unbounded, which will never reach a saturation point.

3. The unity of the Godhead has been extended to humanity, opening the potency of community to spiritually crippled people who can now be fortified by the full potency that is in the Godhead.

4. Satan was wrong and rejecting the potency of unity was wrong, which resulted in his choosing individual life over community life.

5. Satan's self-isolation requires him to turn to the power of might and control in order to survive.

6. The inevitable result of Satan's isolation and control tactics ends in chaos as the only possible conclusion.

7. Therefore, our own isolation is wrong and will end in the same chaos as Satan's.

8. It is possible for two people to bond together in unity and their combined life becomes greater than the sum total of their separate lives.

9. Marital unity between two people in this world catches the attention of heavenly beings, which will never again question the wisdom and superiority of godly unity.

10. The law of reciprocity really works, and labor, management, and business operating under the law of reciprocity can create great wealth and prosperity for all people, changing the way the world does business.

11. Practicing God's principles is like tossing a rock into a still pond, setting in motion wave after wave until the whole pond is transformed from shore to shore.

12. The living Christ can change our inner lives in magnitude, fashioning us into believers who can advance upon the gates of hell and blow them away.

13. Christ is the firstborn of many brothers who become a new race in the world, mirroring God's image and likeness.

14. Every person is the never-to-be-duplicated masterpiece of God.

15. The re-creation of a broken person is an accomplishment of God greater than the creation of the universe.

16. Believers can release gargantuan powers in the world that will result in a changed world.

17. Believers can recapture a runaway church, fashioning a body for Christ that will become a force in the world.

18. A church can expand, overcome, and flourish that does not wait for a God-of-might dominated millennium to succeed.

19. Churches can flourish without submitting to market-driven tactics becoming the best show in town.

20. Followers of Christ can perform in the world much like Jesus who accomplished God's work, and so shall they.

21. The character of God has the potency to capture the imaginations of broken people and entice them upon a journey toward godlikeness and succeed.

22. God's love and forgiveness frees people to journey within, discovering the brokenness and greatness that is there.

23. The image of God has already been woven into the fabric of our beings and is awaiting an awakening.

24. The grace of God has the potency to capture our core, reprogram us for the God kind of life and put away our Sin.

25. It is possible for people to spontaneously submit to the authority of God, allowing Him to direct their lives toward exuberance and fulfillment.

When these truths, along with others, become more than shallow tokens or mere intellectual assent and are embedded deeply within a believer, then that believer can truly believe in the ultimate triumph of God.

The world and Christ's church are approaching the threshold of a Day of Jubilation. The truth has been seen and it has been shown, but the knowing of the truth awaits believers who will pattern this world after the pattern of heaven. Our hearts tell us that Christ is remaking us so we can remake the world. We are not yet finished, so our renewal efforts are clumsy, but we must not give up this hope.

Abraham, Isaac, and Jacob did not give up their hope. God promised Abraham fulfilling life, "And I have picked him out to have godly descendants and a godly household—men who are just and good--so that I can do for him all I have promised" (Genesis 18:19). Abraham did not receive all of his promise, yet he passed on those unfulfilled promises to Isaac. And Isaac passed them on to Jacob, and Jacob passed them on to Joseph's two sons. All of them failed to receive all of God's promise, yet they never gave up hope of a God who fulfills His promises.

God has made a new agreement with the spiritual descendents of Abraham, "But this is the new agreement I will make with the people of Israel, says the Lord: … And no one then will need to speak to his friend or neighbor or brother, saying, 'You too, should know the Lord,' because everyone, great and small, will know me already" (Hebrews 8:10 a and 12). Dare we give up hope of such an ultimate triumph of God?

When basic truths are embedded deeply within us, then our hope will spring to life, and we will be certain that there will be an ultimate triumph of God in this world.

I concede that God's ultimate triumph may not occur in my lifetime, but I say to present and future Cosmic Warriors, "Your kind will eventually overcome!"

EPILOGUE

I served as Chaplain for the Texas Youth Council's Statewide Reception Center in Brownwood, Texas from 1970 until 1975. Those five years of my life were a time of growth in understanding. My assignment was to interview each youth committed by the courts to the Texas Youth Council. I would then write religious and spiritual assessments for each youth. As youths came into my office, I would encourage them to tell their story. They were well conditioned to do this by their experience with community guidance personnel, caseworkers, psychologists, and psychiatrists. They had a story to tell, and most shared their history openly. Their stories revealed abuses that harm and warp sensitive childhood spirits.

Realizing the difficulty with which they might honestly open their lives to me, I began a practice which enriched some of their lives and definitely my own. I would move my chair from behind the desk and sit face to face, with nothing between us except non-threatening space. After hearing their stories, I would agree that they had done a lot of bad things, but this did not mean that they were altogether bad. I would tell them that God made a good person when He made them. The bad things they had done were on the surface, for something had happened inside that had crippled and broken their sensitive spirit. Plainly, I assured them, it was their inner brokenness that had driven them to do the things for which they were now in the Reception Center.

Most of their rehabilitation had been under the guidance of people who urged them to change the way they behaved. I told them that trying to change the outside without changing the inside is difficult, if not impossible. At best they could only achieve partial success, which usually resulted in their living one way, while inside being driven to live another way. I made it clear that changing our inner lives is a difficult assignment, which we are incapable of doing alone.

Next I would tell them the story where Jesus was faced with a religious crowd who had caught a woman in the act of adultery. They wanted Jesus to tell them what should be done with her. Jesus' message stated, "God loves and forgives all His children no matter what they have done." Their national law stated that, "all adulteresses should be stoned." If Jesus said, "Kill her!" He would be contradicting His own message. If He said, "Love her and forgive her!" He would be contradicting their national law.

Jesus was possibly the only person present who saw this woman, as she really was—a woman whose spirit had somehow been crippled and abused so that she was acting out her inner brokenness. The attitudes, snubs, and accusing stares of people had contributed to her self-rejection and self-destruction. Writing in the dirt with his finger, Jesus hesitated a long time before He finally answered their question, "Let him who has never sinned cast the first stone." The condemning religious crowd melted away. Jesus asked the woman, "Where are your accusers?" She looked around and said, "They are gone, (they are not a force now)." Jesus continued, "I don't accuse you either; stop accusing yourself and go to live another way."

Before this incident the religious council had been concentrating upon discrediting Jesus. This was just another scenario, instigated by impure religious leaders in an attempt to discredit and embarrass Jesus further. The next day in their religious council someone said, "Wouldn't it be better for one man to die than for the whole world to suffer?" If this woman had eyes to see, she may have seen that in order to save her from these executioners, Jesus had signed his own death certificate.

I always kept a third chair in my office, which I would pull close to our position, and then encourage the youth to imagine Jesus sitting in it. I would say, "Even though they killed Him, Jesus is not dead. He is alive and His spirit is still with us. He wants to come into our lives and help us to deal with the brokenness that is within us. He wants us to see that we are important to God and loved, but He awaits our invitation for Him to come live in us." Then I would ask, "Do you want to ask Him to come into your life and help you to deal with your broken and crippled spirit?"

This beginning relationship with Jesus should lead a sincere person to exit their comfort zone and begin a spiritual voyage. When they begin this voyage, some marvelous things occur. They begin to be captivated by the character of God revealed in Christ. In their journey they turn the searchlight inward and discover the brokenness within. Yet, in that same inner revelation they see themselves as marvelously made in the image and likeness of God with potential for life like God lives life. Now, they are caught up in wanting to be like God is God and commit to His likeness. Ultimately they begin to understand that God has the potency to capture their wayward hearts (cores) and that He has a cure for their Sin problem. They see that they are no longer doomed to a corrupt heart but can eventually be reprogrammed from the inside out to live life like God lives it. They see that grace has the potency to affect such a core change. Eventually they begin to see that God deserves to be in control and gladly submit to His authority. Now they are under the dominion of God's life-fulfilling principles and begin to bring heavenly life into their present existence. They begin to understand why the servant life is superior to all other alternatives, and they begin to find their niche in some serving ministry. Yet, in their dialogue with God they sense Him saying, "This is just the beginning."

God will not have triumphed until people like this appear in the world, and eventually God's transformed family will prove God's case undeniably, and God's adversary will be bound. In taking this position, God has made Himself vulnerable to us. From this perspective, it appears to be the greatest risk ever taken.

Does everyone have to come to this position for God to triumph? I seriously doubt that everyone will, for the impact of God's family is in the *potency* of those who come to such a position, not in the *numbers* who do. However, there will be a time when every knee shall bow and every tongue confesses that Jesus' kind of life is supreme. Those who do not respond to God's love may limit themselves to another kind of existence. Yet, even there the Father's love continues to pursue them, but they may have destroyed their own capability of responding to it. The sting of hell is to forever lose the ability to respond to God's love. Those who are unmoved by God's loving grace fasten themselves to an existence that cannot enjoy the eternally expanding kind of life. "God, forbid!"

In the motion picture, *Man of La Mancha*, as Miguel de Cervantes and his companion, Sancho, begin to ascend the stairs to appear before the Spanish Inquisition, they breathlessly look into each other's eyes, and Sancho, who once was plagued with timidity and fear, whispers to Miguel de Cervantes, "courage." I would echo Sancho's call to all Cosmic Warriors, "courage", for your kind will eventually overcome.

ABOUT THE AUTHOR

I was born and reared in central Texas. I completed undergraduate studies at Rice University in Houston, Texas in 1958, and completed theological studies at Southwestern Baptist Theological Seminary in Fort Worth, Texas in 1962. After graduating from seminary, I studied under Dr. Nat Tracy at Howard Payne University in Brownwood, Texas— auditing his undergraduate courses for several years. Dr. Tracy and I served together as co-chaplains at the State Juvenile Rehabilitation Center in Brownwood, Texas for five years.

I was pastor of three churches in central Texas before founding an experimental house church on Lake Brownwood in 1968. This made it necessary to become a bi-vocational minister. This church pioneered in providing outdoor worship services for visitors to Lake Brownwood. Church by the Lake focused upon spiritual formation and experimented with various spiritual growth techniques. I remained the spiritual leader for Church by the Lake for 26 years until my partial retirement in 1995.

My bi-vocational ventures were residential home building for 25 years. My wife, Pat, and I constructed and operated a mini storage business in Bangs, Texas for 20 years and have operated a hunting ministry in Colorado for 35 years. I led in the formation of a partnership to purchase and operate a small ranch in Colorado. Until recent months I served as managing partner for this venture.

Pat and I have been married for 54 years. We have two sons and 3 grandchildren. In our partial retirement, we served as International Service Corps missionaries for the International Mission Board of the Southern Baptist Convention. I led in the construction of a building for the Nampula Bible Institute in Mozambique. Pat assisted the strategy coordinator for Mozambique. Together, Pat and I hosted short-term American volunteers coming to Africa to engage in various volunteer mission projects.

Writing has been a long time interest for me. I wrote and published my daily meditations via the Internet for 5 years. I see myself as a work in progress with promises to keep and miles to go before I sleep.